The Change¹¹

Insights into Self-Empowerment

Jim Britt ~ Jim Lutes

With
Co-authors from Around the World

The Change[11]

Jim Britt ~ Jim Lutes

All Rights Reserved

Copyright 2016
The Change
10556 Combie Road, Suite 6205
Auburn, CA 95602

The use of any part of this publication, whether reproduced, stored in any retrieval system or transmitted in any forms or by any means, electronic or otherwise, without the prior written consent of the publisher, is an infringement of copyright law.

Jim Lutes ~ Jim Britt
The Change[11]

SKU: 2370000350466

Co-authors

Craig Wayne Boyd

Bob Heron

Gina Gardiner

Jerry M. Tolle, Sr.

Anna Horst

David Grossman

Kelli Locatelli

Janna Hoiberg

Marco Valerio Ricci

Joy Humbarger

Kimberly Zink

Michael Cole

Renee Dean

Carolyn Rivera

Colleen Williamson

Crystal Areal

Todd Mauney

Devani Freeman

George Lynch

Kasey Higbee

The Change is proud to support Good Women International

Every five minutes, one American child (many as young as ten years old) will be abducted and trafficked into the sex trade. 274 children a day, 100,000 each year and that estimate could be low. The total current number of human trafficking victims in the U.S. alone reaches into the hundreds of thousands and worldwide into the millions.

All profits from the sale of Amazon Kindle electronic books are being donated to Good Women International, whose focus is on the prevention of sexual exploitation of young women and children. They support self-empowerment and educational programs worldwide designed to educate our youth to avoid becoming a victim. A recent successful project was an anti-trafficking curricula for our high schools which is now complete and being utilized in many high schools around the world.

Enslavement is a reality. It is documented and it is real. The question is: What are we going to do about it?

To make a donation to Good Women International, a non-profit subsidiary of Village Care International, go to: www.SupportGoodWomen.com. All donations are tax deductible under Tax ID #: 88-0471768. We welcome and appreciate your donations, no matter how small.

http://GoodWomenInternational.org

Note: *Donations are never for salaries, as Good Women is a volunteer organization.*

DEDICATION

This book is dedicated to all those seeking change

Foreword

Berny Dohrmann,
Chairman of CEO Space International

To The Readers of *The Change* Series:

Jim Britt has been a mentor to *Chicken Soup* authors, and to some of the foremost thought leaders on earth. Jim Britt's groundbreaking work in *Letting Go*, releasing past traumas and betrayals in life to return once again to forward-looking manifestation within your full powers, has been instructing at leading *Fortune* companies and to standing-room-only seminars all over the world. For three decades, Jim Britt has been the "trainer of the trainers," of which I am only one. Jim has been an instructor at CEO Space, the most prestigious, hard to get into faculty on the planet, where he developed millions of dollars of resources as he assisted others to develop tens of millions of dollars for their own dream making. Jim is the most "unchanged by success and wealth" man I have ever known. He is an unselfish archangel, like in his book *Rings of Truth*.

Today, Jim Britt and Jim Lutes, along with many inspiring co-authors from around the world, bring a pioneering work to the market to transform your own journey into master manifestation. Their principles are forged on coaching millions on every continent. As you read, you are exploring self-development as the world has yet to practice. In fact, Jim and Jim's publications lead to this one APEX MOMENT. Everything you have done to date in your own life, everyone you have met, every lesson you have learned, has led you to this one GREAT life opportunity… the moment of your own transformation into ever-rising full potentials.

As a five-time best-selling author myself, as a filmmaker, and with CEO Space, you can imagine how fussy I am to write a foreword to publications in the self-development space. CEO Space was just ranked by *Forbes Magazine* as the leading entrepreneur firm, which hosts five annual business growth conferences serving over 140 countries. It was also named by *Forbes* as THE MEETING in the world that YOU CANNOT AFFORD TO MISS. The world today demands more than a reputation defender to secure your forward brand; it requires that you take responsibility for your own brand and reputation in life. This book will inspire you to do just that.

CEO Space International has supported launches for many amazing works, including Chicken Soup for the Soul; Men Are From Mars, Women Are From Venus; Rich Dad, Poor Dad; The Secret; No Matter What; Three Feet From Gold; Conversations With The King; and now the movies Growing Up Graceland and Wish Man (for Make a Wish Foundation); Outwitting the Devil by Napoleon Hill and Sharon Lechter; Tony Robbins' great publications; of course Jim Britt's best-selling book Rings of Truth; and so many more. The totals have reached more than 2 billion eyeballs! You can't play around with that Mount Everest of credibility that I guard like a bank vault!

You can therefore appreciate why I encourage 100% of our followers of all the publications named to BUY JIM BRITT and JIM LUTES' book series *The Change* as a customer recognition for your own ten-best close relationships or clients. But don't just buy this book; rather, I endorse that you buy 10, and you giftwrap them to acknowledge your most important top ten relationships in life or clients in business. By doing so, you will retain more clients and encourage repeat buying. You may also receive more referrals and strengthen each relationship. The laws of giving will come back to you 10 to 1. When you give freely, you will always receive a rain into your life just as you rain into the lives of those you treasure. Jim Britt, Jim Lutes, and the insightful and inspiring co-authors have given you in *The Change* series a great opportunity… more important than pouring ice water over someone's head on YouTube as a challenge for charity! The gift that keeps on giving begins when you step up and BUY 10, knowing you have been instrumental in inspiring 10 friends to live a better life. Together, we are going to reach 1 BILLION SOULS as we help Jim Britt, Jim Lutes, and their co-authors to achieve their goal to transform human consciousness in our lifetime. Like Zig Ziglar, Jim Rohn, the great Roger Anthony, and so many friends who have passed, my friend Jim Britt is now a historical event in every training, every publication, and every online work at CEO Space. If you ever have the opportunity, STOP YOUR LIFE and see JIM BRITT & JIM LUTES LIVE and you will thank me personally, I know.

Their work is powerful. You'll let go of the baggage you've been carrying around for years and learn to embrace everything that creates the future you want and deserve. As you close the pages of any of *The Change* books, you will say over and over again "THANK YOU Jim Britt and Jim Lutes for creating this work." You will gain a new life of super focus as never before and you will commence to master manifest in your own individual life as never before. *The Change* books provide tools to transform results for corporations, institutions, and individuals, and once applied it will be impossible to miss your future success in life.

In my opinion, there are only the following areas to embrace for each of us:

Spiritual oneness and balance

Recreational balance and nature

Relationship where *Perfection Can Be Had!* (my book)

Career attainment of goals that you, yourself, reset along the way

Parenting either directly or by embracing a child you adopt to mentor at any and every age in life

These perspectives come into alignment within the framework of Jim Britt and Jim Lutes' imagination, along with decades of human-potential work. My advice is this work is a "BUY 10 TO SHARE WITH FRIENDS" pledge. In fact, a billion readers is a global path that Jim Britt and Jim Lutes are going to achieve NEXT for the world common good.

Let's help in this quest, as both men unselfishly donate their only asset, their precious LIFE TIME, to elevate one life at a time to their full potential and greatness.

My final request to all those who are reading my foreword is that you DO IT NOW. When you think of the good you will be doing, just ask yourself, "How long will I make them WAIT?"

I'm buying my 10 today!

Berny Dohrmann

Chairman, CEO Space International

P.S. I so approve this message for all my readers and followers worldwide. CEO Space has helped authors break the book of all records a half a dozen times, which means the only record to beat can be done with the publication you are buying 10 of now. Together, we are going to set a global record with one publication. Make the PLEDGE and give the gift of personal development. DO IT TODAY!

Table of Contents

Foreword vii

Jim Britt 1
Reinvent Yourself—Every Income Level Requires a Different You

Jim Lutes 19
The Blank Canvas

Craig Wayne Boyd 29
I'm Still Here

Kimberly Zink 39
The Only Sales Formula You Will Ever Need

Devani Freeman 49
Miracle Mindset: A Guide On How to Dream Bigger, Achieve Extraordinary Results, and Live a Life That Lights You Up

David Grossman 63
How Better Communication Can Improve Your Life: The Top 10 Must-Dos

Kelli Locatelli 77
LIFE: What I Signed Up For

Kasey Higbee 89
Nay-sayers be damned!

Anna Horst 97
Conscious Empowerment

Colleen Williamson 107
You—The Unfinished Masterpiece

Janna Hoiberg 115
The Effect of Attitude on Altitude

Todd Mauney 125
A Dichotomy for Prosperity: "Breathing In" and "Breathing Out."

Carolyn J. Rivera 137
Are You Nearsighted or Farsighted in Your Personal Vision?

Michael Cole 149
How to Get Anything You Want by Using the Magic of NLP

Gina Gardiner 157
Genuinely You: Discover how to live a happy, confident, and stress free life starting today!

Joy Humbarger 169
Leading the F____!! Out of Change

Renee Dean 181
Success Starts With Loving Yourself

Crystal Areal 191
The Seven Day Habit

Bob J. Heron 201
The Power of Self-Influence

Marco Valerio Ricci 211
Everything Is Perfect as It Is: How to create a plan and forget it to reach an extraordinary life

Jerry M. Tolle, Sr. 223
How I Became the Boss at 10 years old

George Lynch 237
The Diamond Kid

Afterword 247

Jim Britt

Jim Britt is an internationally recognized leader in the field of peak performance and personal empowerment training. He is author of 13 best-selling books, including *Cracking the Rich Code; Cracking the Life Code; Rings of Truth; The Power of Letting Go; Freedom; Unleashing Your Authentic Power; Do This. Get Rich-For Entrepreneurs; The Flaw in The Law of Attraction;* and *The Law of Realization,* to name a few.

Jim has presented seminars throughout the world sharing his success principles and life-enhancing realizations with thousands of audiences, totaling over 1,000,000 people from all walks of life.

Jim has served as a success counselor to over 300 corporations worldwide. He was recently named as one of the world's top 20 success coaches and presented with the best of the best award out of the top 100 contributors of all time to the direct selling industry. He also mentored/coached Anthony Robbins for his first five years in business.

Jim is more than aware of the challenges we all face in making adaptive changes for a sustainable future.

Reinvent Yourself—Every Income Level Requires a Different You

By Jim Britt

Once again, that uncomfortable feeling pays a visit, but this time you can't close the door and just ignore it. The discomfort that you are feeling is with yourself. You feel like your life does not fit you anymore, and maybe it hasn't for a long time.

But do you dare reinvent yourself? Do you have the courage to take the necessary steps to let go of the person you are today, and used to be, so that you can blossom into the person you have always wanted to become? This can sometimes feel scary because you have to let go of attachments to the past, and what was, in order to reinvent the new you.

If you are up to the *reinventing yourself* and ready to travel along a new path to where you have never been, now is the perfect time to get started, and I want to help.

The process of reinventing yourself is very empowering. You might not realize it yet, but you do have all it takes to truly ignite change. Don't let anybody else tell you otherwise.
The first thing you need to do is take a look at yourself. What do you want to change about yourself?

Since you are starting over, so to speak, if you are going to dream, you might as well dream big. Think of yourself as an author who is writing your new life story. You are limited only by your Imagination.

Before you start reinventing yourself, you have to at least know what you're working with and what you want changed. The more specific you are, the better. This will give you direction and allow you to focus on the right things.

If you ask someone what the most important thing in their life is, most often they will answer "family" or "their health." But is that actually true? When you look at where the average person spends most of their waking hours, it is focused on making money, so money must be the most important area for most. So let's discuss money.

What's the secret to incredible financial success? The secret is, there is no <u>one</u> secret! The reality is there are many "secrets" that work together in combination with one another, giving you the winning "combination" to succeed financially!

Think of success like a giant vault at the bank with a thick steel door blocking it and a combination lock. Unless you have the right combination to that lock, it doesn't matter how much you beat on the door, how hard you work, how many lists you make or good intentions you have, because there is a combination you must know to unlock that door and get it to swing open so you can walk through to the other side where the money is being held, waiting for you.

Many years ago, I met a very wealthy person and I asked what inspired him to be wealthy. His answer really surprised me. "Money is a game and the man with the most notches on his belt wins." I was shocked! I was a young man at the time and having grown up without much, I wanted to become wealthy. Yet after hearing this person's response, I looked deeper into his eyes and frankly, he didn't seem all that happy and the sense of lack of balance in his life was apparent. He was out of shape and had a look in his eyes of anxiety, loneliness, and anger. I could tell that he had stepped on a lot of people to get to where he was.

How about you? Do you think that being financially wealthy takes putting yourself first and trampling over those that get in your way? Do you think that being wealthy means putting the lust for money ahead of everything else?

On the other hand, I've met very wealthy people who give back to their community, have large circles of friends, and always seemed

The Change[11]

to be abundant in so many other ways. In fact, a year or so ago, I took a camera crew around the country and interview 12 self-made mega-millionaires and one billionaire. The requirement was that they all had to have started with nothing. In other words, they didn't inherit their wealth. And all 12 made their money in different industries…internet marketing, traditional business, real estate, television, direct sales, social media, etc. If you asked any of these 12 individuals the same question, you'd likely get this sort of answer: "wealth is simply a vehicle that magnifies your deeper personality traits and mindset."

The following is what I have learned from my own experiences, the experiences of these 12 mega-millionaires, and others I have associated myself with over the past 40 years.

Wealth is the ultimate power of leverage. Nothing is truer about becoming and deciding to become wealthy. It is a magnifying glass into your money mindset.

Wouldn't it be nice if you could simply decide to become wealthy and you did?

Well, let me fill you in on a big secret…you can!

You already know the basics. You know that you should pay off your debt and start budgeting. You know that all you need to do is regularly invest money into your savings and let time do the work. Spend less, save more, build your investment portfolio…you've heard it time and time again. Then why aren't you on the way to becoming wealthy?

There are many reasons that people don't take action, even though they have the information. The reality is that so many people are just simply afraid to change. Fear takes a lot away from a person. You know you don't want to fail, but when you buy into fear, it will take you down that path.

Here's one key to the vault combination lock. For things to change for you financially, you have to make a change; otherwise, you'll continue to keep producing the same results you've been producing. Now, this may come as a shock to you, but most people really don't want to change. Just give them a beer, point them toward the sofa, and give them the television remote. They will continue to complacently live out their lives complaining about what they don't have.

Most people are much too busy earning a living to become financially free. They spend the majority of their time focused on what they *don't have* and what they *don't want*, on how to pay the bills, instead of focusing on what they *do have* and what they *do want* in their lives.

I know people, as I'm sure you do, that love having the drama of being up to their ears in debt. It's a balance beam that keeps excitement in their lives. It's a roller coaster ride that is thrilling, but always drops them off at the same place time and time again. And at such a huge cost! What they don't realize is that they can't maintain their balance or thrill forever. At some point, you have to decide where to get off…or you fall off at the end.

One of the things I discovered in my 40-year career is that successful people think differently, and they do things that the majority of people are not willing to do. Most have been conditioned to believe that creating wealth is difficult, or that it's only for the lucky few. They convince themselves that "someday" they are going to be a success, to start their own business, to make a financial plan for their future, to have all they want in life…someday.

Someday…what an interesting concept. Think of all the things that were supposed to have happened by now…that someday that you may have convinced yourself was just around the corner. To most, that someday is where we've convinced ourselves we would be right now, if only we had more time, more talent, more education, more money, or maybe a better opportunity available.

Before going any further, I would urge you to stop right now and take a realistic look at your last five years. Have you truly made progress? Are the last five years what *you* wanted? Are you where you thought you'd be today financially? And, most importantly, do you have a solid plan for the next five years?

Too many people like to complain, but really just don't want to make the effort. They don't have time. They'll do it next year. Let me tell you, you have to find time to get your financial situation in order if you want to gain wealth. Time is costing you money. The more time you spend trying to pay off credit cards, the more you pay the credit card company and contribute to their wealth.

I'm not saying to ignore your financial obligations. What I'm saying is that paying off your credit cards, although a good place to start, will not bring you wealth. Why? Because after you pay them off you are still left with the mentality that charged them to the max in the first place.

You *can* have all the money you want. It just takes learning and developing the traits that rich people use, and some time to make it happen. If you want to change your financial situation, you have to reinvent yourself, because the old you won't cut it.

To become wealthy, you will need to develop a number of vital traits. It's the number sequence to the vault.

First is a firm decision to become wealthy. Wealthy people you'll find make solid decisions and commit to seeing them through. Those who are not financially successful put off decisions or mess around with their decision once it is made.

Mediocrity cannot be an option. A decision creates a mindset, and a mindset makes you as mechanical and predictable as a calculator. Hit this number and it appears on the screen.

I'm not talking about deciding "how" to make the money. Decision comes first, then the how to.

It's really surprising though how many people fear making that decision. They do all sorts of things to keep the moment of decision at arm's length, including: Gathering more data. Getting ready to get started. As soon as I have my plan complete. Getting others' opinions. Fretting over who the decision might offend. Worrying about the resources needed to pull off the decision. Or hoping they'll just get lucky and make the money they need without making a decision, etc.

The real problem is that most are stuck in a comfort zone and making a decision would mean having to do something different that might be a bit painful or at least uncomfortable. That's a decision we all face…the pain of staying stuck in our current situation or the pain of changing it. Most people would rather live with the "old you" for fear that becoming the "new you" would be too painful. If that's you, then stop reading now.

Let's say a person makes a decision to be wealthy. What happens next when the old programs, the old habit patterns, and old mind chatter kicks in? "Wait a minute! What makes you think you have the talent to become wealthy?' "I've never done it before! Maybe I really can't become wealthy." "I don't have the expertise, time, money, education, etc. to become wealthy." And before long, all the "self-talk" has pulled you off course and changed your decision into something totally different from becoming wealthy.

I remember a fellow named Bob who had created a hair care line to go into drugstore chains. He had the connections to get it into the stores across the country. However, after months, the line just wasn't selling.

Instead of just giving up, a business associate convinced him that he should sell it on a TV infomercial. This was one of the first, if not the first, TV infomercial ever produced. So nobody knew if it actually would work.

Bob was a decision maker and a doer, so he said let's try it. That decision turned into over $200 million in sales that netted him almost $100 million. The point is, he could have given up with his first attempt.

One of the mega millionaires I interviewed went bankrupt three times and today has a net worth of over $250 million.

My point is that you don't give up just because one approach to becoming wealthy didn't work. There are thousands of ways to become wealthy, but without a wealth mindset, nothing happens.

Remember this: <u>every income level requires a different you</u>. You have to reinvent yourself for each new income level. You have to be willing to let go of the "old you" and embrace the challenge of becoming the "new you." And, if you want to learn, grow, and change, you have to hang around people that challenge you to become a better you. If you want to become a million-dollar-a-year earner, but yet you hang around and take input from people earning $60,000 a year, you'll likely to be right where they are financially.

I know people, as I'm sure you do, who go to work every day to a job that they hate. They hate what they earn and/or what they do, but they stay because they feel they have no other choice. They justify their position by calling it job security. But what they don't realize is that there is no security in most jobs! It's called *prolonged poverty* in my book!

It's like living in a place you hate, but you're afraid to move because of your job. Then you lose your job and can't afford to move, so you look for another insecure position that will keep you in the place you hate. *That's a sort of insanity, don't you think?*

What would I say to a person in that position? "If you want to get better, you have to make better decisions, and you have to hang out with and take input from those who've done it." I would say "if you want to be rich, you have to stop working for someone else's goals and dreams and make a decision to start working for your own. You have to stop with the employee mentality, reinvent yourself, and start thinking like wealthy people think."

The first step is to make the decision, one that doesn't allow for anything less. Up until the decision is made, nothing happens...except, of course, the decision to stay where you are now. In reality, not making a decision is a decision to leave everything status quo.

The next trait all wealthy people have in common is that they are bold. Financially successful people have learned that action is vital. And often times that requires a level of boldness. They know that procrastination kills. They live with the reality of consequences and know there will always be uncertainty in decisions, but they boldly step forward and make the decision anyway.

No one can see all possible ramifications; no one can predict every contingency; no one can absolutely prevent failure. The wealth-minded person knows that failure is not final—it's just one of those possible outcomes that happens on their way to success.

The real danger surrounding decision making is not "will I make the wrong decision" but "did I make the best decision possible given the facts and circumstances." Success-minded individuals invest in learning what they need to make the correct decisions from those who have done what they want to do.

But, when it comes to investing in mentorship, so often I hear people say "I can't afford it." "It costs too much." When in reality, they can't afford not to. Because without mentorship, it costs way too much! Wealthy people look at value, not cost. What will the investment make them, rather than what will it cost them?

The real question is, "what do you really want?" Are you just dreaming about success or standing on the sidelines observing other people's successes and wishing you had what they have? Do you justify why you aren't financially successful? Or are you bold enough to step out in the spotlight and take center stage before you have all the answers?

The real questions are: "Do you really want to be rich?" "Do you want to retire wealthy?" "What would financial success look like to you?" "Do you want to have a residual income that covers all your financial needs?" Most people have never defined what financial success would be for them, and they've never made a decision to have it. And that's the only reason they don't have it!

The three most important questions that you can ask yourself are: one, have I defined what financial success means to me? Two, am I basing my future financial success on past experiences? And three, am I willing to reinvent myself to have what I want? How you answer those questions can change your life!

Often times, there is a feature in the investment section of some Sunday local newspapers. It's a success story column on people who've made it big financially in a respective business. You can also find those stories in magazines like *Entrepreneur* or *Inc*. You'll find stories of individuals who have carved out a niche for themselves in selected fields, lived a fulfilled life serving others with their skills, and amassed quite a fortune while doing so. You'll always find one common trait in all the featured personalities. Not one of them. Not some of them. But this trait is in all of them! It's called a "wealth mindset." Despite the fact that they're from different backgrounds, all of them possess the same mindset when it comes to money. Wealthy people think differently. This is the infamous "money consciousness" that most of the motivational and personal development trainers speak of so often in their books and seminars.

This wealthy mindset basically means this:

Regardless of the physical condition that you may currently be in, as long as you see yourself bathing in financial abundance, your actions will maneuver and circumstances will unfold in a way to create the wealth that you see yourself enjoying. If you possess the wealthy mindset, you will have the "Midas" touch when it comes to earning money. If you don't, you won't. It's that simple. The fortunate thing is, all of us possess the innate ability to fire up this wealthy mindset. But the key is letting go of the old you and holding true to the new you that you want to become.

First is making the decision to be wealthy. Second is being bold. Next is letting go of your limiting beliefs about money and changing how you relate to money.

Some people frown at the mere mention of money. How many times have you heard people say something like this: "Oh, I'm not doing this for the money" or "Money isn't everything"? Well, they're not wrong. Money isn't everything. The fact is that money in itself has no value. It's the things that money can buy when in circulation that makes it so valuable. Money can buy material possessions, personal freedom, and we all deserve to have what we want.

At the same time, if you look from a different angle, once you've got enough money to be financially free, it can literally change what you do from laborious work to spending more precious moments with your family and friends as well as doing the things you love. In essence, if you never come to terms with what money can bring forth into your life, its real value, your uneasiness with the "idea" of money will limit your ability to create more of it.

To put it simply, just imagine this: would you go into a car showroom if you've never had the intention to purchase a car? You may not want to buy it now, but the fact that you walked into the showroom implies that you appreciate the value of what a car brings. It can serve as a means of transportation for you and your family. And because of the perceived value you see to owning a car, you'll find the means and ways to get one. Having money is the same. Once you see its value and believe you can have it, you'll find the ways and means to getting it.

Remember, you can't create something that you're not in harmony with or that you haven't decided to have. Therefore, it becomes imperative that you really get this wealthy mindset concept before you move on to other steps. You should definitely have a conversation with yourself, or someone that can mentor you, to let go of the beliefs, if you have some, that are limiting your ability to have more money.

Having money means…finish the sentence…

What came up? Do you feel your answer will move you toward being wealthy?

Answer these questions:

Why do you deserve to be wealthy?

What do you believe about money?

How did you come to believe this?

Who taught you to believe that way?

Were they wealthy?

Who taught them?

Is my money mindset based on past experiences or beliefs?

The only way to change a belief is to challenge it. A belief is something that you have decided is true…it may not be at all. A belief is simply a decision that something is true. The good news is that you can change a belief simply by changing your decisions, making up something new, and letting go of the old you.

If you want to be wealthy, you have to first decide to be wealthy. Whatever being wealthy means to you. Another number to the combination to the vault is to decide "why" you want to be wealthy. What's the payoff for wealth? Your "why" is the fuel that will take you where you want to go. It's the passion behind the decision.

Everyone has the right to be wealthy. You have the right to be wealthy….and yet, most allow a temporary lack of money to eat into our minds, literally confining them to the vicious cycle of mediocrity. The bottom line is that people are poor because they have not yet decided to be wealthy. To put it another way…mediocre earners are mediocre earners because they have decided to be.

So long as you make a conscious decision to become wealthy and have utmost faith that you can achieve it, and you let go of your outdated beliefs and change your relationship with money, you will act accordingly to what you believe. Why not say "yes" to getting wealthy today! And say it with conviction.

Deciding to be wealthy only gets you started on the quest, but what sustains you throughout the journey is the "why" you want to be wealthy and letting go of the mind chatter that pulls you back into your old habit patterns.

What is the reason that you want an extra $1 million in your bank account or you want to earn a million dollars a year? If you do not have a burning desire supporting your reason, and you don't let go of your old way of thinking and believing, you'll find your inspiration tapering off sooner and your decision fading into something totally different to being wealthy. That's the trap that most everyone falls into.

Try this exercise. Take a piece of paper and scribble down all the reasons that you can think of why you want to be wealthy. Maybe you'd like to retire earlier and travel around the world? Or you want to quit your job and be a full-time parent? Write down as many why's as you can think of. Needless to say, the one that resonates with the deepest part of your heart should be written on an index card to remind you of the outcome you desire.

You'll also want to determine what wealth is to you. How much you want will inadvertently determine the action that you'll need to set forth to reach it. Again, wealth can be whatever you say it is. For some it might mean 10 million in the bank. For others it might mean having enough residual income coming monthly to completely cover their overhead. For example, if it's $5,000 per month that you're looking for, working in your existing job and going for a raise in pay might suffice. However, if $100,000 per month is what you intend to achieve, other alternatives such as starting your own business, investing in properties, or working on your "skills sets" to better serve the marketplace will probably be more effective. More importantly, knowing how much you want prepares your mind for the potential issues you may face to make that happen.

The challenge therefore becomes: how do you know how much you want? Arbitrarily quoting a figure will probably do you more harm than good. If the amount you pull out of the sky is much higher than what you really want, your approach to acquire the wealth may not be in harmony with your "why" and you may end up burning yourself out. In the event that the amount is less than what you really want, then you'll find yourself re-adjusting your "why," which may not inspire you to keep going. Again your "what," your "why," and your "mindset" need to be in harmony.

Suppose you want to get from point "A" to point "B." There's route 1, route 2, route 3—all the way to infinity. When you believe that there's only one way to get there, it limits your possibilities. When you are totally open to how to get there, the mind starts considering the many options and may prompt you to act on one of them that you haven't even thought of before. Along the way, your wealthy mindset may allow you to recognize different opportunities, encouraging you to change course and go through a totally different experience than originally planned.

I remember Steve, who attained wealth in a totally different manner than expected. Initially, his plan was to market his own music compositions through conventional methods. But he instead stumbled upon online internet marketing and embarked on an unconventional route to becoming an internet millionaire. It was not an easy route, as he had to juggle learning about the new internet marketing model—about which he knew nothing—while still working a full-time job. But his burning desire to be rich got him through the hurdle to financial freedom.

Start to imagine yourself as already having wealth. Before you physically acquire the wealth that you've envisioned, you need to own it as if you already possess the amount of money that you desire! How would you feel right now if you were wealthy? What would you be doing differently? How would your life be different?

How would your day unfold? Start to "own" the result of your wealth now! The subconscious mind is unable to differentiate between actual possession and mere visualization. So by imagining that you already have it, you're encouraging your subconscious mind to seek ways to transform your imaginary feelings into the real thing.

I know many people refute this type of thinking as impractical. But if you think about it, isn't everything around us a true manifestation of someone else's imagination? Everything man made was in someone's imagination before it was created. And when they possessed the passion to create it, the ways and means appeared. The Wright brothers imagined being able to fly and the reality is, we are now able to fly in an airplane from one country to another in a matter of hours. Thomas Edison imagined lighting a whole room using a single source and as a result, the lightbulb was invented! Yes, it took a few tries—about 10,000—but eventually he created it.

Look around right now. If you are in a room, look at all the things in that room that made someone wealthy. Why not you? Take a walk outside and look around. How many things do you see that made some else wealthy? Why not you? It all started in someone's imagination. They owned it first in their mind before it became a reality. It's a fact that without the imagination of great visionaries, we would not be able to enjoy many things that we enjoy today. Radio, television, automobiles, and thousands of other great inventions we would not enjoy today if not for someone first imagining them into existence. Decision comes first, then the answers!

You too possess the same capability to create and improve your own destiny by constructing it in your mind first. All improvement in your life begins with the improvement in your mental pictures. Change your mental pictures and you change the outcome of your life, like changing a movie in a DVD player.

For example, you can imagine receiving income checks when you open the mailbox every day. Or you can picture yourself receiving an award for being nominated the best entrepreneur in your country or having a best-selling book. Not only does it send the message to your subconscious, it serves as a great form of daily inspiration.

It is absolutely essential to have a crystal-clear picture of what you want to accomplish before you begin. If you want to attain wealth, you must learn to operate with a sharply defined mental image of the outcome you want to attain.

Focus your attention on the spot where you want to land, not on where you are now, or on any misconceptions or shortcomings you may think you have. In other words, visualize your arrival and you'll develop a magnetic harmony with the ways and means required to get there. Solutions will begin to appear and obstacles will seem to disappear. Answers will come to you. People will show up to support you in your endeavor. Look at the end result as something that you are already prepared to do, you just haven't done it yet.

Think about this. Your success is something that you have been preventing; it's not something you have to struggle to make happen.

You'll find the solutions taking you toward your goals will come to you in the most unexpected and sudden ways when you let go of the old you, reinvent yourself, and embrace the new you.

You don't need the *perfect* plan first. What you need is a *perfectly* clear decision about your success and the right mindset, and the ideal way to get you there will materialize. You can't get all the answers upfront, so don't waste your time trying. The success formula doesn't involve getting everything neatly organized, with everything in its proper place and sequence and all the risks eliminated before you make the move. If you want that, then get a 9-5 job, but realize that will never make you wealthy. Get a target…point, then take action!

Your true greatness lies within your ability to decide what you want and a commitment to having it, and then taking bold action to get it.

The world you have perceived in the past is the world you now live in. The world you perceive now is the world you will create in the future. And the world you create is limited only by your imagination, your mindset, and your ability to let go of the old you and reinvent the new you.

Everyone has the right to be wealthy. You have the right to be wealthy. Yet, most allow a temporary lack of money to eat into their minds, literally confining them to the vicious cycle of mediocrity.

The bottom line is that people are poor because they have not yet decided to be rich. So long as you manage a conscious decision to become wealthy and have the utmost faith that you can achieve it, you will act accordingly to what you believe.

We create our own reality. A person who believes that the universe is abundant and they can attain whatever level of financial success they desire…and a person who believes that money only comes from working hard and will receive money only from hard work…are both right. Each will have many experiences to prove that their "belief" about abundance is a "fact."

However, the good news is…you can change your belief and therefore change what you experience.

I help individuals to get clear about what they want, why they want it, and to locate and let go of the mental and emotional blocks and programming that is stopping their success. The results I produce have won me the honor of being named as one of the top 50 and the top 20 success coaches in the world. I'd love to work with you.

***

To contact Jim:

www.JimBritt.com

www.PowerOfLettingGo.com

www.CrackingTheRichCode.com

www.FaceBook.com/JimBrittOnline

Jim Lutes

Having taught his branded form of human performance since the early 1990s, Mr. Lutes has accelerated top-level entrepreneurs throughout his career by conducting trainings on personal growth and subconscious programming into worldwide markets.

During this time, Jim took his skills regarding the human mind, and combining it with trainings on influence, persuasion, and communication strategies, he launched Lutes International in the early 1990s. Based in San Diego, California, Jim has taught seminars for corporations, sales forces, individuals, and athletes. Having appeared on television, radio, and worldwide stages, Jim's style, knowledge, and effectiveness provide profound results.

"Jim Lutes possesses a unique ability to create performance change in an individual in a fraction of the time it takes his competitors." The core of human decisions are based on the programs we acquire, reinforce, and grow. Combining Jim's various trainings, individuals can reach new levels of achievement and fulfillment in all areas of life. The results are at times nothing short of astonishing.

The Blank Canvas

By Jim Lutes

We are all born of pure spirit. Our subconscious mind is the gateway to the universe and connection with the divine. Intuition is like the conversation between 'ourselves' and universal consciousness. When we talk of being intuitive and accessing intuition, we are talking about using that part of the subconscious mind that *is* Universal Power. This happens when all of our 'parts' are in alignment.

We are all equals when we are first born—regardless of what kind of family or situation we are born into, the truth is we are still vulnerable, pure, needy babies. Our minds are like a blank canvas, ready to learn and grow and not pre-programmed in any way. At this stage, we are residing in a pure and innocent state, if you will. We soak up knowledge at a fast and furious pace in the first months and years of our lives, as our canvas becomes painted on with the impressions of our parents or caregivers, guardians, other family and other authority figures in our lives. Consequently, as we soak up knowledge and imprinted programming from our parents and everyone else who affects us, our intuition is weakened, and our connection to the greater subconscious mind of the entire universe is lost. We are conditioned to rely more on external factors and cues in our environment then we are on our *internal* environment.

What starts out as the blank canvas quickly becomes crowded with programming, right from the minute we are born. There are three primary ways our minds get programmed as we grow up: traumatic experience, authority figures, and repetition.

When you experience trauma as a child, your subconscious creates a response at the time that's primary goal is keeping you safe. For example, perhaps when you were four years old, you burned your hand on the stove. This trauma and memory became stored in the subconscious and as you grew up, you knew not to put your hand on the stove. A more extreme example might suggest that you even became afraid of the stove as you grew older. Sometimes the trauma is no longer kept in your memory at the conscious level and you don't know why you have certain fears. You might have a strong fear of being in small spaces. What you may not even remember is an incident from your early childhood wherein you were contained in a small space and you were terrified. Programming from trauma is often forgotten by the conscious mind as people age, because of the emotional powerhouse traumatic incidents are. Our innate nature is so concerned with keeping us protected and safe that we may develop very strong emotional responses as a result of traumatic experiences. You can always find out what programming is running in your subconscious mind that came from trauma by working with a qualified hypnotist or psychotherapist.

The other way we become programmed is through the authority figures in our lives. Our parents are usually the major players here. However, it can be anyone that was influential on your life as you grew up. For lots of people, if there are limiting beliefs or thoughts around money, chances are they came from the authority figures and the words they heard these figures say that they took in. If you grew up poor and always heard your father say, "Money doesn't grow on trees!" it is possible that you may grow up hoarding your money or believing you will never have enough. If your parents always asked you to be quiet or did not even invite you to speak at the dinner table as a child, you may have taken in the message that your feelings don't matter and you continue to keep quiet as you grow older, only to find that as an adult it keeps you from making presentations at work or limits you in other ways. The voices we hear growing up impact our subconscious minds in profound ways, and one could argue these have the strongest influence on what we believe about ourselves and the world. Again, the old internal-versus-external struggle. In contemporary Western society, we are much more encouraged to give more importance to the external messages, as opposed to listening to what our internal messages (intuition) are saying.

The third common way we are programmed is through repetition. Any words, comments, behaviors, or actions that were repeated to you as you grew up became entrenched in your subconscious mind, for better or for worse. A good example of repetition is the media. If you think back to all the messages you received as a child growing up—all of the gender messages, messages about how you should look, even how you should be if you want to "fit in," all of these are repeated over and over again through media programming, particularly television. These messages are usually reinforced by our family, authority figures, and society. If you don't believe you were programmed by television as a child, think again. For men and women, there are probably millions of cases of people struggling with low self-esteem as a direct result of images in the media of unattainable bodies and looks for the greater majority of people.

Whether this programming came to us as a result of traumatic episodes we faced as children, or from the voices of the authority figures in our lives, most of us grew into adults entirely unaware that there had been any programming altogether. The reality is, as you grew up, the authority figures—and even the media and other influential voices—helped you create parameters in your life, for example, the need for approval and the fear of criticism may have led you to slowly lose your individuality over the years, without your being consciously aware that it was happening. It's a subtle process that can effectively erode any 'authentic' or 'true' sense of self.

Instead of following your heart, you found yourself following the masses without ever fully understanding why. One day you arrived at the realization that you are dissatisfied, unhappy, and not fully self-expressed on the path you're living. In short, you recognize that you are living far under your potential. Yet chances are, even if you arrived to that point, you were still unable to comprehend why you felt that way or what hidden forces may have been at work to lead to that moment. You may not recall the specific words spoken by those around you that you absorbed as you were growing up, but they are affecting your life even now through the emotions that show up when you are involved in certain situations. Negative statements of any kind, like "you'll never amount to anything", "no one in our family is rich", "it's no use trying", "you will fail", "life is one big struggle", and so on were far more dangerous than those who uttered them could have anticipated. For these statements dug grooves in your subconscious mind, the repercussions of which persist throughout your life unless you learn to overcome them. If you have ever wondered why you felt anxiety or fear when you tried something new, or despair every time you look at your finances, chances are these emotions have arisen as a result of a belief being triggered by an earlier experience that you were not aware was still influencing your behavior. Are you beginning to 'see' how much your original blank canvas has been painted on by other people's ideas and influences?

If people only knew how influential their words are on their babies' minds, we would see a radical shift in the way we parent. The programming we received, especially in the earliest years of our lives, has a profound effect on who we are and the choices we make today. This is not to be used as an excuse to justify why you are stuck, or in bad relationships, sickly, or financially unstable. Rather, just recognizing that you began with a blank canvas that was subsequently influenced and programmed by everyone around you is an essential first step in moving you forward. You cannot move forward in life into the aligned and positive human you wish to be, manifesting all that you desire, without recognizing the areas your mind has been imprinted upon from an early age. This is a crucial ingredient to making lasting change and using those changes to fuel the life you desire to create.

We are born the same, all of us, coming into the world as babies with open and empty minds. As we grow up, we assimilate cultural norms, we assimilate the fears of our parents and other authority figures, and we assimilate the need for approval or fear of criticism, which can translate into the loss of our individuality. Have you ever felt out of alignment with who you really are? Chances are if you dig deep enough into your subconscious mind, you have some story

The Change

in there that was put there by someone of authority in your life, and it's a fear of rejection, or a need for approval, or any other fear or idea that would contribute to you hiding your real self from the world. Somehow, you learned it was not safe to be an individual, particularly the individual that you really are, and this learning has led you to where you are now. If you are stuck and out of alignment, feeling like one of the masses and locked into a 9-5 job while your heart screams for freedom and the ability to work for yourself, take a look at what conditions you grew up in, and whose voices and thoughts you heard most. If we humans only knew the influence we have on one other, we would help each other to grow positive subconscious thought patterns, not limiting ones. Imagine what kind of world we would live in if this were the case.

Another way to look at this is to think of your mind as a nightclub. When you were a child, there was a bouncer at the door who let everyone in. You did not have a filter yet—in this case, a bouncer who was discerning. So everyone came in—negative thoughts, negative memories, positive thoughts, lessons learned, basically any and all experiences, both positive and negative. Everyone and everything got into your nightclub from the moment you were born. Now imagine that as you grew older, the bouncer decided to start to be more discerning about who is already in your nightclub. You might try to allow a new positive, affirming thought into your nightclub, only to find there is a nightclub full of negative memories, beliefs, and other thoughts that are crowding out the positive thoughts you are trying to re-populate your nightclub with.

As you start to change your life by changing your thoughts, it is imperative that you kick some of those dancers out of the nightclub. If you don't make space in the nightclub for some positive thoughts—or new thoughts at all—those thoughts cannot stay, because the nightclub is so full of negative thoughts. What happens next? You need to empty the whole nightclub, evict the negative thoughts and limiting beliefs, and start to only let the positive and affirming thoughts in. Does this make sense? The bouncer needs to wake up and actively guard the nightclub to only allow in those thoughts and beliefs that serve you. We go along in life and we often don't even want to see the occupants of our nightclub, sometimes going so far as to engage in self-medicating behavior so we can stay in denial. Many of us are afraid to "see" who has been populating our nightclub. Somehow, a lot of the negative thoughts and beliefs that got into the nightclub serve us and have served us through the years, helping us to survive. Many of these thoughts and beliefs become patterns and give us a sense of safety and predictability, even though many of them are no longer helpful in our present lives. Just because our nightclub is populated by ideas and thoughts that previously helped us to navigate experiences in our lives, it doesn't mean they need to stay on! And, to boot, they are not the best dancers in the nightclub either!

While we are the chief creators of our lives, these patterns and much of our early conditioning may have led us to a place of feeling stuck, negative, or dissatisfied with our current lifestyle. Imagine for a moment that your life is like a car. Would you give the wheel to people you did not know or trust? Would you let a person who repeatedly crashed the car be the chief driver? No, of course not! Beginning to recognize and examine these negative thoughts, patterns, and beliefs will enable you to become the driver in your life. Paying attention to your thoughts moment to moment will empower you to navigate the terrain of your life with more skill, ease, and harmony.

Our subconscious mind absorbed everything when we were growing up; our canvas filled up quickly, whether we liked it or not. Now, as adults, it's important to dive deep into our subconscious minds to filter out all of the limiting beliefs—beliefs that perhaps once served us, long ago, but that certainly no longer serve us or our greater purpose in life. It's time for the nightclub bouncer to put his foot down, by being more selective and choosey about who is allowed to come into the nightclub. (Hint, you are the bouncer!)

It is incredible how common it is when people begin to reassess their lives and their relationships, with themselves and others, or the success they are having (or perhaps not having), they discover that much of what has been negatively affecting their lives, their achievements, their finances, their careers, their intimate relationships, and even their bodies was influenced by their parents. Not only have our parents programmed and imprinted their beliefs and patterns upon us, but we also developed strategies to cope with our living situations, the other side of this double-edged sword. As we grew up and tried to be liked, approved of, or appreciated by one or both parents, we developed behaviors, beliefs, and patterns to help us meet those needs. In many cases, the decisions people have made from childhood onward were about avoiding the pain that was inflicted on them by a parent or loved one. So we can be forty, fifty, even eighty years old, and we are still living the strategies we lived as children. We are effectively re-living the lives of our younger selves in a cycle of unconscious repetition.

As if these things weren't enough to leave us limited as adults, for many of us, as we grew up, we often told ourselves "I'll never be like that!" when referring to our parents. Yet here you are today, quite possibly exactly like that. You don't want to admit it, but if you watched a film of your interactions, you might say "Oh dear, I never wanted to be like that parent," yet you are. Or, if you didn't become the parent you said you would never become, you may have gone in the entirely opposite direction, and you are not like that parent at all, but now you are something else. You are the opposite of the extreme you didn't like. Now you are another extreme, but that doesn't work either. Conventional society fails to teach us how much our early conditioning affects us; it becomes part of our subconscious and we don't even see it. It stays within us and remains part of the invisible fabric of our thinking and our decision-making every single day.

Remembering the essence of our true selves, and the starting point we all shared and came from, can help us as we try to eradicate obstacles that keep us from achieving our goals in life. We are pure spirit manifested into bodies. We are not solely bodies and mass, lumbering through life, waiting for life to happen to us. Each of us is designed as an autopoietic being. We are in fact creators, with Universal Power readily accessible to us through our subconscious mind. We have the capacity, through our thoughts, to create every minute of our reality, and yet so many of us don't know this, don't believe this, or don't know how to fully implement this. I want you to learn how to tap into this potential, to your inherent creative potential.

For all of us, our minds never really stood a chance. For centuries, our ancestors have passed down their thought patterns and beliefs, imprinting beliefs both positive and negative on each subsequent generation. Even your parents did not fully know what they were doing when they imprinted upon you all of the programming that you integrated from birth. They were just doing the best they could with what they knew. Often, our parents were themselves repeating the conditioning that they experienced in their own families.

There may be no preventing this programming or imprinting; however, as adults, you can reverse the programming by using world-class subconscious mind programming techniques such as those that are outlined in this book. Once you are aware of how much your subconscious impacts your conscious mind, you will seek out ways to overcome these thoughts, the ones you never chose, could not have chosen, and, really, had been chosen on your behalf. These techniques help you to separate yourself from the emotion, which is really what makes the thought real to your subconscious mind. These strategies, in effect, will help you erase and re-paint your canvas, so that the memory and content remain, while the emotion dissipates. The subconscious mind responds to visuals and emotion, and by disconnecting the emotion from the thought, we can move forward into changing certain areas of our lives that may once have been limited by these thoughts and the strong emotions they generated.

While it is impossible to revisit the blank canvas our minds once were in our lives, it is possible to reverse the damaging effects of all the negative thoughts that filled that canvas. It is possible to reprogram the subconscious mind, and it is possible to grow your intuition so you can truly see the divine connection within, the connection to all of creation.

***

To contact Jim:

Email: info@lutesinternational.com

Websites: www.lutesinternational.com

www.jimluteslive.com

Craig Wayne Boyd

Rooted in the Southern tradition of country music and topped with a rebellious flair, Craig is an extreme talent who excelled at singing and playing the guitar at the age of four. He received long-due critical and mainstream recognition as the Season 7 winner of *The Voice*. Taking the title as a member of Team Blake (Shelton), Craig dazzled the audience with the premiere performance of "My Baby's Got A Smile on Her Face," which debuted #1 on the Hot Country Songs chart, becoming the second song (following Garth Brooks' "More Than A Memory") to ever do so.

Growing up in the Dallas, Texas suburb of Mesquite, Craig's childhood was highly influenced by gospel and country music and he later became the choir director at his hometown church. After a trip to Nashville, life-changing events came his way. Craig signed a publishing deal with EMI and after several years of prolific songwriting, he began touring heavily, logging more than 1,000 shows in four years, and opening for acts like Jamey Johnson, Randy Houser, and Brantley Gilbert. In 2015, Craig opened up for Rascal Flatts during their *Vegas Riot!* nine-show residency at the Hard Rock Casino in Las Vegas before continuing on his headlining *West Bound and Down Tour*.

I'm Still Here

By Craig Wayne Boyd

A wise man named Bob Speir once told me, "Life is made up of all these tidbits; what you do with them and how you use them is what dictates the rest of your life, so concentrate on the small things." For me, those tidbits always had something to do with music. It's always been a part of me. I grew up surrounded by music… whether I was singing in my church choir, school plays, listening to music, or completely devoting myself to learning the instruments I picked up at garage sales. I knew music was in my future because I couldn't get enough of it. Which musical path to take was something I struggled with early in my life. As the son of a honky-tonk player and a mother who raised me to sing gospel, I was constantly conflicted until the pastor of my church explained to me that you can't always preach to the choir and to go where I was led.

I wasn't sure what all of that meant until I was 23. My father and I traveled to Nashville where I was fortunate enough to meet a very prominent person in the music publishing scene and play a few songs for him that I'd written in Dallas. He told me I was on the right track, but that I had to be present to win and then he asked if I was willing to move to Music City and start a new journey. I never thought twice about it. I said *"Yes,"* surprising myself with my complete lack of hesitation. On the way home, I looked up and asked, *"God, is this what I'm really supposed to do?"*

> *We can sometimes question ourselves out of our dreams, not realizing it. After all, I'd just built a new house, I was married, and I had a stable six-figure job... was I going to do this and did it even make sense? The answer came to me like a 2x4 across the forehead when I pulled up to my house and found a note from my then*

> *wife. She had left me, along with specific instructions not to try to find her.*

Shortly thereafter, I became extremely depressed. I lost my sales job and one rainy night in Texas, I rolled and totaled my truck. Being told I was lucky to be alive, I wasn't feeling very *lucky,* but I knew that God had given me my answer. Six months later, I was on my way to Nashville with everything I could pack in the back of an old farm truck my father had loaned me.

After moving to Nashville, it seemed as if I was on my way to fulfilling my dream. I was writing with some great songwriters, performing in writers' rounds, and formed the trio, Southland, with musicians Cole Lee and Levi Sims. A year later, I landed a publishing deal with EMI, one of the most renowned publishing companies in the world. For 3 years, life was good. The trio was getting positive attention, we had labels interested in us, and we were playing packed venues. You know if there's one thing the music industry will teach you, over and over again... don't hold your breath. Before I knew it, my trio had broken up, I had lost my publishing deal, and close friend and former bandmate, Levi, had passed away from cystic fibrosis. I was back to square one, grieving the loss of my friend, and trying to figure out how to pick up the pieces. Bob's words would swim through my head—"tidbits, and what you do with them, concentrate on the small things." I hung on to these words.

After much contemplation, I decided to pursue a solo career. I took the heartache of the last few years into the studio and recorded an album to reflect the highs and lows of my life. I found new band members and hit the road... playing gigs from Minot, North Dakota to Key West, Florida and everywhere in between. I was introduced to a new independent label in Nashville and we recorded another album to reflect the *determination* that I had to finish what I started. The single from that album was a direct reflection of my journey so far; aptly titled, **"I Ain't No Quitter".** We even made a video and submitted the single to radio where it began climbing the charts. Finally, I was back! The single reached the top 30's on the Music Row Charts, defying the precedent at the time that if you weren't on a major label, it was nearly impossible to get a song played. I was determined to break the Nashville mold and be an independent artist with a hit single. I'd been playing nearly 250 dates a year, including a radio tour where I visited every radio station that would have me. And don't hold your breath again! When I returned from one of my radio tours, I saw movers pulling furniture out of my independent label's office. My immediate thought was, "Awesome! We're getting new furniture," but the reality was that the company had lost its funding. Even with my single still moving up the charts, I was headed back to square one once again.

> *No label, no money to pay band members, no gigs, and back to the drawing board. It was 2012, strike three.*

I'm not sure if it was my "stupidity" or "stick-to-itiveness" that kept me going, but I know most sane people would have packed it in and given up. By now, I was a new father to my first child, a son named Jaxon, who had become a new inspiration in my life. It wasn't just about me anymore and I had the pressing responsibility to be successful and do what I knew to do to support him. My current single, *"I Ain't No Quitter",* was supposed to define me and yet there I was, standing at a crossroads, trying to decide if I had the strength to move forward. The answer was yes, because ***I was not a quitter and I would find a way to figure it out***. I started over again and for 2 years I played as many gigs that I could on the road, supplementing income wherever I could to support my son. I picked up jobs working construction while also writing and performing as often as possible. I will never forget this one day in particular, I was working on a job site when a Nashville label executive came into the house we were building and recognized me. He looked at me and asked, "Aren't you Craig Wayne Boyd? What are you doing here?" I told him I had a son to support now and needed to pick up some extra work. I've never been ashamed of who I am, and don't get me wrong, hard work has never been beneath me, but in this moment, I truly felt defeated. This isn't where I wanted to be—it was where I had to be.

> *I began questioning God's plan for me… was music really the route I was intended to pursue? Had I already used up all of my chances or was there another lesson, another road I had to travel to find my way?*

My landlord had just given me 30 days to move out and it seemed like I was being pushed in another direction. Nearly homeless and out on the road, I'd just had a heart to heart with my drummer about quitting music and concentrating on another career. I didn't want to give it up, but I needed something stable so I could confidently support my son. With quitting on my mind, I opened up my computer, only to find an email from a producer of the NBC TV show *The Voice*, asking if I would be interested in auditioning for Season 7 of the series. I thought it was spam. Turns out, it wasn't. After debating whether or not I wanted to be in a televised singing competition, I felt this opportunity must have been put in my path for a reason. The challenge was mentally preparing to head to L.A. With no official place to call home, I spent the weeks leading up to my audition packing up my things, moving them into storage, and sleeping on any sofa available, in hopes that something would come of this next venture. *This is when I decided if this didn't work, I would have to give in to quitting, which I dreaded.*

> *"To me it was never a competition against other contestants, it was more of a competition against me and my own inner demons telling me I couldn't do this."*

When I arrived in L.A., I began questioning everything about myself. Was this how I wanted to further my career? Was I cheating the system? But with much soul searching, I decided that finding the best way to achieve your goals is not cheating; it's changing your way of doing things and thinking outside of the box. If this was the opportunity that was being laid out before me, then I was going to do my best, no matter what the outcome. During one of the many vetting interviews, **_I was told by one of the producers that I was "positive to a fault."_** That was funny to me because little did they know the internal battle going on inside me. No matter what, I couldn't let anyone else know how distraught I was because I knew positive affirmation was the only way I was going to move ahead. With my mind focused on doing _"my very best,"_ I flew through the audition process, landed on Blake Shelton's team and was paired up for my first battle. I knew this was a contest against other people on the show with the object being to beat the other artists... but to me it was never a competition against the others. It was more of a fight with myself and my own inner demons telling me I couldn't do this. When the first battle was over, I stood in front of my coach and was not chosen to move on. Rejection is not fun for anyone, especially when it's nationally televised, but I looked inward and knew I'd done my best. As I was about to walk off the stage, knowing if this was the end of the road for me, then I could accept it and move on to that next chapter of my life, the lights flashed, buzzers went off, and I was saved by Gwen Stefani, another coach on _The Voice_. Relief flowed through me as I realized I'd been given another chance to prove I belonged there.

They say, "If you wanna hear God laugh, tell him your plan"! Apparently going home was NOT on HIS agenda. The following week, I was put up against another artist on Team Gwen. I was once again defeated in the 2nd battle and about to step off the stage when the lights went off, the buzzer sounded, and Blake Shelton was stealing me back to his team! I can't explain the rush of emotion I felt in those 30 seconds between being rejected by Gwen and then saved again by Blake, but if I had to try, it would be like falling off a cliff and right before you hit the dirt, something swoops in and catches you. You don't know if you're crying because you're still reeling from the fear of falling or the relief of being saved.

> Reflecting back, connecting the dots, it was the same thing that had been going on in my life prior to the show. Only this time, it was on television in front of millions of people, in a shorter amount of time, *but* with the same outcomes. I was denied, then saved, denied and saved again. The challenge ahead would not just be to prove myself to my coach, but to the voting public…. Little did I know that I already had.

As the show went "Live" and the viewers were able to decide my fate, I pushed on as I always did, keeping faith in myself that I was doing the right thing from week to week. The struggle wasn't in the choice of songs or how I would perform them—that part was easy because I'd been doing that for 10 years prior. It was in the seconds before my name was called to stay, wondering if America understood me or if they would decide I fell short of their expectations. The fans never disappointed, they never wavered. So, as true as they were to me, I stayed true to myself. Time after time I challenged myself never to focus on the other contestant's song choices or if I could beat them. I made many friends, offered advice to whomever asked, and helped them out in their performances. I knew the outcome would be whatever was meant to be.

The weeks flew by and I found myself at the moment of truth. It was down to the final Top 4. As I was walking through the set, someone yelled "Hey! There's Craig Wayne Boyd!" and without thinking, I responded *"Yep! I'm Still Here!!*

> *In that moment, it hit me. All my life I lived in that moment of the song, "I Ain't No Quitter" I'd released to radio all those years back and now I was living its sequel. Never giving up,*

> *never giving in to those demons that constantly nagged at my subconscious telling me I couldn't do it and I knew I needed to write that song. I took pen to paper and began writing.*

Those who know my story and those that watched Season 7 of NBC's *The Voice* know the outcome, but to touch briefly on that moment; I remember being on the stage with the last 4 contestants. I was the only member left from Team Blake and the other 3 were from Team Adam. We huddled together on the stage in front of a live audience as the results slowly whittled our numbers from four to two. I watched Damien walk off first, then Chris, wondering how it was possible that I would be left to stand alone with Matt. Once again, would my hopes be dashed? I'd never set out to win the show. I had come here to prove to myself that I could stand with the best and that I was worthy of being here. There I was, in the final moments, and suddenly I wanted it so badly. Although I could accept second place…would this be the moment I was triumphant? Or would it turn out like every other time, where I reached up, and could feel my dreams within my grasp only to have them slip through my fingers? Would I have to "tuck my tail" and run back to Nashville to start all over? Would I have to take another career path to support my son? Where would I live? If things had gone differently, my guess is that because of my determination, I would have found a way to stay with music in some form or fashion. That's the way I was taught. It was bred in me to be that "nose to the grindstone" type of guy, and I knew I still had more fight in me.

Call it luck, call it fate, call it divine intervention, but as it turned out, I didn't have to worry about any of those questions. My name was called and I was crowned the winner of Season 7 of *The Voice*. In that moment of realization, I thought back to Bob Speir and his wise words for me when I was 17:

Each point in my life when my dreams were shattered, I pulled some knowledge from his statement as I would pick myself back up and move forward. Each challenge, each disappointment, each victory was a tidbit I kept with me and learned from to make the next moment better. I never realized how powerful his words were until then. I knew as I held the trophy in my hand, confetti falling around me and tears in my eyes, that I had conquered a mountain by simply believing in myself... and so begins a grand new journey and the next chapter of my life. What will it hold?

I'm Still Here
Written By:
Craig Wayne Boyd, Arlis Albritton, & Josh Helms
I'm a believer, but there's a song in me that's begging to be heard
Yes, I'm a dreamer, hanging on to hope for everything its worth
So I skipped a few meals and slept in my car
When you're down that low they don't care who you are
In this who-do-ya-know town
Oh but look at me now
I'm still here
Standing strong
Giving it my all
Cause that's just who I am
I won't give up
I don't know what that means
It's not inside of me
To pack my bags and turn my back
Walk away just like that and disappear
I'm still here

The Change[11]

I'm no leaver, but I gotta be where the marquee holds my name
Because I'm a singer, so I move town to town and stage to stage
But my son's at home and he's too young to know, why sometimes daddies have to go
So I point to his heart and say, son, if you ever need me, right here's where I'll be
I'm still here
Standing strong
Giving it my all
Cause that's just who I am
I won't give up
I don't know what that means
It's not inside of me
To pack my bags and turn my back
Walk away just like that and disappear
I'm still here
No, I won't give up
I don't know what that means
It's not inside of me
To pack my bags and turn my back
Walk away just like that and disappear
I'm still here
I'm still here
I'm still here

***

To Contact Craig

Website: http://www.craigwayneboyd.com

Facebook: https://www.facebook.com/Craigwayneboyd

Twitter: https://www.twitter.com/cwbyall

Instagram: https://www.instagram.com/cwbyall

Snapchat: Cwbyall

YouTube: https://www.youtube.com/Craigwayneboyd

Kimberly Zink

Kimberly Zink is the CEO and President of Klemmer & Associates, an international leadership and character development company. Their client list includes Aetna Healthcare, General Electric, Walt Disney Attractions, Hewlett Packard, and many other manufacturing firms, medical clinics, banks, as well as distributors from over a dozen network marketing and direct sales organizations, and thousands of individuals. After careers in insurance and network marketing, struggling to make ends meet as a single mother with enormous debt, Kimberly walked into the seminar rooms of Klemmer & Associates. Within a year, she not only paid off her debts, she also created over six figures in income and is a millionaire today using the tools she learned in those seminars. Now she facilitates seminars worldwide. Her message is simple: You have the power to experience a large amount of change in your life in a short period time. Her dynamic, raw, and authentic style has catapulted her to the top of her field. If you are looking for truth and the tools to experience real change and move your business, finances, and relationships forward, Kimberly Zink is a woman you want to know.

The Only Sales Formula You Will Ever Need

By Kimberly Zink

Would you like to increase your sales? How many of you just instantaneously thought, "I'm not in sales!" Well, if you have ever gone on a date... guess what? You made a sale! You either "sold" the person to ask you out, or you "sold" the person to say yes. Have you ever gotten your children to do their homework when they didn't want to? If so, then you made a sale! Have you ever gotten a job? You *sold* your employer on your skill set and your ability to do the job.

The truth is, each and every one of us are in sales. What we are selling differs from person to person. A sale is simply communicating in such a way that empowers another to take action. Empowering others to take action is about creating a real desire in others to do something because they see the value in doing it, not because they were manipulated.

So, knowing that we are all in sales at some level, would you like to increase your sales? Maybe you want to create deeper, more intimate relationships. Perhaps you want to create more finances or increase the size of your business. In this chapter, I am going to give you the only sales formula you will ever need.

The key to this formula is making your sale from a place of enrollment. For me, enrollment is motivating or inspiring someone to do what you want them to do, because they see the value in doing what you want them to do for their own reasons and not out of compliance or manipulation. When you can truly enroll someone into a sale, they are buying because they want to. They are buying because they truly see value in what you are offering. They are buying because they are enrolled in you.

Have you ever purchased something, and then left feeling like it was pushed on you? Or left feeling like you "had to" buy it? No one likes feeling that way, and no one likes making someone feel that way. Many people shy away from selling because they do not want to "twist someone's arm." Selling does not have to feel slimy and it does not have to be hard. It doesn't have to be that way! In fact, the beautiful part about this formula is that when it is put into practice, your customers will leave the sale feeling fulfilled and excited that they made the decision!

The ultimate sales formula is called "Want-Problem-Solution." There are three steps to using this formula and they must be used in the correct order to be effective. First is what we call "want." You need to find out what the other person wants. When most people sell, they start with what they are selling first. They are so excited to tell people about what they have to offer that they forget to ask the human being in front of them what that person really needs or wants. I suggest that is exactly the opposite of what you want to do! The absolute first thing you are going to do is find out what the other person *wants*.

Step 1: WANT

When my son was younger, his teachers told me that he was having trouble reading. I knew my son loved to have fun and be busy. Needless to say, sitting down to learn to read was not his favorite activity. I also knew that trying to force him to comply or to try to manipulate him would not be very effective in the long term. He would resist. We have all heard the phrase growing up, "Because I'm your mother and I said so!" Did that ever inspire enthusiasm or motivate you?

I knew I needed to "sell" or enroll my son in learning to read. One day, I asked him about how learning to read was going at school. He told me, "Mom, I don't think I need to learn to read." I said, "Okay, so if you are not going to learn to read, what do you want to do when you grow up? What is your dream?" He said, "*I want* to play football." Once he told me what he wanted, I had something to work with. As soon as I knew what he wanted, I could have a conversation to enroll him in learning to read.

Most people trying to sell something immediately start telling someone what *they* want or what *they* have and how that can benefit the listener. Think about a time in your life when you have been desperate to make a sale. In that time, what did you talk about or ask for? Most of the time, we worry about ourselves first. It is easy to forget to find out what others want or need when we are knee deep in our own needs. If you want to be a successful enroller or excel at sales, become an expert at finding out the needs and wants of others.

Putting others first and finding out what they need or want is a continuous practice. If you want more intimacy in your marriage, find out what your spouse desires. If you want to create more sales in your business, find out what your prospects want. When you become an expert "need/want finder," you will increase your sales dramatically! Start learning what others need or want and how to fill those needs and wants and you will have more of what *you* want in *your* life than you know what to do with.

When you start to truly ask people what they want or need, they might not immediately know the answer. Or, you might be met with some resistance. This is a new concept for a lot of people, so be patient and diligent at the same time. Be genuine in your request. This is not about manipulation; it is about being of service. When people know that you are sincere, they will generally start to open up. Think about how you react to someone who spends an entire conversation talking and not really listening to you. What is your reaction?

Step 2: PROBLEM

The second step in this formula is called "problem." What is your client's problem in getting what they say they want? There is definitely a problem or obstacle for them; otherwise, they would already have what they say they want. The key to this piece of the formula is they must be the one to identify their problem so that they have the *experience* of their problem.

One of the reasons that our seminars are so powerful is that we work in experiential learning. We suggest there are two ways to learn something. You can learn through repetition, or you can learn through emotional involvement. Repetition can be a great way to learn, and it can take a very long time for something to become second nature. On the other hand, when you have an *experience* of something, you have an instantaneous revelation and dramatic shifts can happen right then and there as a result of the emotional involvement in the experience.

For example, let's take wearing your seatbelt in a car. It takes repetition at first to remember to wear your seatbelt every time you get in the car. But, if you were in a car accident, you instantly have a different feeling about wearing your seatbelt and you put it on automatically because you learned the value of wearing a seatbelt through the experience of the accident.

Our seminars are set up for you to have your unique experiences so you can create your own revelations and find your own answers, not someone else's experiences or answers. Many times, if you have an experience out in the world, especially negative or painful experiences like the example of the car accident, you learn and also discover that the prices you pay for the choices you make are a lot higher than you want to pay. We create a safe environment in our seminars for you to have experiences so that you can learn the lessons quickly without paying high prices for the knowledge.

So again, for the "problem" piece of the formula to work, your client needs to identify their problem so that they are emotionally involved. The truth is that you don't know what their problem is, and if you start guessing, that's all it is; a guess. You may have an idea, but unless they identify it, you will never know if it will resonate with them or not. Have you ever had someone try to tell you what your problem is? It doesn't work very well, does it? If they are having trouble coming up with what their problem is, just be in conversation with them until they make a few guesses, and land on what the problem is for them. Again, this is about being of service to the other person. Listening from a place of sincere curiosity will greatly increase your success, regardless of the relationship.

Back to my son; when I learned that he wanted to play football, I got excited for him! I told him to grab all his football stuff and that we were going to go in the backyard a start practicing. He ran upstairs and came down with his football and his playbook. I grabbed the football, he opened the playbook, and he discovered his problem. He flipped through the pages and looked up at me with big eyes and said, "Momma, I can't read it."

Step 3: SOLUTION

Once your client has identified their problem, you now have the *opportunity* to apply the third piece of the formula. You get to share exactly what it is you have been waiting to add; your solution! When my son looked up at me and identified his problem, I knew the solution was at school with his teachers. But now, instead of me *telling* him that he had to pay attention to his teachers, he was enrolled in why he wanted to learn to read, and I had made a sale!

This third piece of the formula is all about you telling the other person about why your solution gives them what they want and need and solves their problem. Piece by piece, you are going to show the person you are working with why or how your solution solves their problem and gets them what they need or want. It is almost as though there is a hallway of doors, and together you are closing all the doors except for the one you want them to walk through. If they are slow to walk through the final remaining door, you may need to turn up the temperature in the hallway. Otherwise, it is possible they may become too complacent in their current situation and never choose a door. This is known as "the Ask."

Some refer to the Ask as "closing the deal." This is how most people view sales. They only know the Ask and it is why they are uncomfortable with sales. If you sincerely connect with someone, the Ask is as natural as can be. Sincerely connecting with someone simply means applying the first two steps in the formula by *listening* to them with your full attention in such a way that they know they are being heard. If you passionately believe in what you are selling, including yourself, and you are acting out of integrity and you are sincere in your belief that your product, service, idea, is the best solution, you have made a sale!

Actually, they have made the sale, as they have *enrolled themselves in your solution.* This sales method will create better results because all you are really doing is giving someone what they told you they wanted.

This is all of course if what you have to offer gives them what they want or need and solves their problem. If at some point in the conversation you realize that what you have to offer does not solve their problem, then point them in a direction that is going to support them. You will gain their respect through your integrity and a long-term relationship is now possible, including future referrals. The more you help people with the solutions to their problems, the more successful you will be.

The Want + Problem + Solution formula truly is the ultimate sales formula and the only sales formula you will ever need. You can create massive success when you listen to people, identify their wants and needs or what's important to them, and then help them solve their problems or overcome their obstacles, or help them achieve what is important to them. Master this formula in all your relationships and you will flourish in all areas of your life!

LANGUAGE FOR ACTION

At Klemmer & Associates, we also apply the formula using "Language for Action." There are four steps in Language for Action. The first step is identifying someone's want, or desire, through what we call a *conversation for commitment.*

CONVERSATION FOR COMMITMENT

Everyone wants to know what's in it for them! This is where the conversation for commitment comes in. Conversation for commitment is all about identifying what motivates the person you are actively enrolling. Motivation varies, but there are three main motivators that motivate most people. If you are stuck trying to find what motivates someone, try these three options.

MOTIVATION 1: MONEY

Money is a key motivator for a large percent of the population. The amount of money may vary from person to person, but most everyone gets excited when given the opportunity to earn more money.

MOTIVATION 2: RECOGNITION

Money alone does not motivate everyone. Some people are highly motivated by recognition. You might know someone who is motivated by recognition or you might even be someone who is motivated by recognition. Someone motivated by recognition might want a parking spot right up front with their name on it; some want a fabulous title; others appreciate an award presented to them in front of the entire company.

You can get creative with ways to give a person recognition. The key is that it will generate motivation for them that would outweigh any discomfort or objection to what you are asking them to do. Many people might, out of a sense of humility, say they are not motivated by recognition. For some that might be true, but ask what their reaction would be if someone else received recognition or credit for their work and achievements. What would your honest reaction be?

MOTIVATION 3: CAUSE

The third motivator is the most powerful. It is cause. People do extraordinary things, both heroic and horrible, for a cause. Some give their lives to save others, like soldiers save their comrades' lives by sacrificing their own, some fly airplanes into buildings. Forgive the graphic example, but it certainly makes the point: People will not do those things for money or recognition, but they will do them for a cause. Find someone's cause or purpose and you will know how best to motivate them.

The entire first step of this concept is having a conversation for commitment to find out what motivates the person you are in a relationship with. This is one way to find out what people *want*. When you find out what motivates people, you can enroll them.

THE REQUEST or "ASK"

Once you have a conversation for commitment and find out someone's motivator, you can move to the next step, the *request*. A true request must give the other person the opportunity to say no. If they are not able to say no, you have compliance or manipulation, not commitment. Commitment and compliance create incredibly different results.

A request also has three key components, it needs to be *specific*, *measurable*, and have a *timeframe* attached. You need to be able to measure whether your specific request has been completed by the agreed upon deadline.

THE PROMISE

The third step is the *promise*. If someone says yes to your request, you are in agreement. You have a promise. If the response to your request is no, it is not rejection; it is actually great feedback and simply means that you have not found their true motivator. Simply go back to the conversation for commitment to find out what the person truly wants.

THE FOLLOW-UP

The forth and final step is crucial; *follow-up*. If the deadline is Friday at noon, show up, rain or shine. Do not miss or renegotiate your follow-up.

During the follow-up, ask three simple questions: What worked? What didn't work? What's next? The questions are the same whether or not the person accomplished the request. Anytime the results are not as expected, go back to the conversation for commitment to find what truly motivates that person.

Language for Action is based in Want + Problem + Solution and vice-versa. You can create great change and massive success when you start connecting people in a sincere effort to learn their needs and wants and helping them fulfill them.

Don't just trust me that this formula works...test it! My mentor and the founder of Klemmer and Associates, Brian Klemmer, always told me, "Base it on results. Often harsh, always fair." This is one tool from our seminars—put it into practice and experience real results.

If you are thinking you cannot create success in your current circumstances, pre-order my book, *I love me not, I love me*, set for release in late 2016. It's the true story of my early life and how I chose to change my thinking, my choices, and my life. It is the story of my triumphs over situations that I could have chosen to paralyze me and would have been great excuses for living an unfulfilled life.

Please visit our website or call our office to find a seminar we are offering near you.

***

To Contact Kimberly:

Kimberly Zink

1-800-577-5447

www.klemmer.com

https://www.facebook.com/klemmer.associates/

https://www.facebook.com/kimberly.a.zink.1

https://www.youtube.com/user/KlemmerMedia

Devani Freeman

Devani Freeman is a social media marketing expert, online business coach, mindset mentor, and boutique agency CEO. She has helped hundreds of heart-centered female entrepreneurs build their audience online with ideal clients, and get known as the go-to expert in their field, so they can make more money, achieve freedom, and make a difference—all from modern marketing strategies that work.

She does this by showing them, step-by-step, how to effectively and authentically grow an online following and master their mindset to create wildly successful results.

With over 8 years in traditional and digital marketing, Devani has created proven strategies that allow entrepreneurs to create a loyal, engaged, and eager tribe online, full of people who can't wait to work with them. In addition, Devani runs a boutique Social Media Marketing Agency offering done-for-you services for busy business owners who want their Social Media and Facebook Advertising taken off their hands.

Miracle Mindset: A Guide On How to Dream Bigger, Achieve Extraordinary Results, and Live a Life That Lights You Up

By Devani Freeman

Have you ever wondered *what is the secret to those that achieve extraordinary results in their life*? People that just seem to be able to easily dream big and live a life that fills their soul up?

As I write this chapter, I am sitting at a local coffee shop in sunny San Diego thinking about how blessed I am at this moment. I have a thriving business that provides me freedom, deeply meaningful relationships, and an impact in the world.

But it's been a crazy journey. One filled with miracles, challenges, and more miracles (thank goodness).

You see, everyone has a story. Everyone has a journey that has brought them to where they are today.

Most of us experience miracles along this journey—but we don't even realize it.

Miracles can be experienced as a feeling of being in flow. Like being at the right place at the right time.

Webster's Dictionary says a miracle is: a surprising and welcome event that is not explicable by natural or scientific laws and is therefore considered to be the work of a divine agency.

Well, let me start by saying that my life has been nothing short of miracles. I experienced my first awareness of a miracle when I was 19 years old.

I remember it clearly. I was fresh out of high school and enrolled in beauty school. I was also addicted to meth at the time. Yes, you read that correctly, *addicted to meth.*

But I wasn't the strung out meth addict. No, I was actually the polished and perfect straight A student, BUT with a huge secret I was hiding from the world.

Inside I was closed off, sad, disconnected, and insecure, as I didn't know how to handle moving from a big city to a small town at the ripe age of 14. I was thrown into a new school where I felt outcast and alone. I was bullied by some of the girls at school and eventually began homeschooling.

In my attempt to find community and connection with others, I met a new group of "friends." This new group of friends introduced me to my new best friend, meth.

When I was on meth, I felt alive, I felt confident, I felt a rush of energy like never before. But as we all know, meth is deadly. I was slowly killing my body.

So there I was in beauty school. I was attempting to do a beauty service on a client and I had an encounter that left me feeling confused. Something basic that I didn't understand. I had an inner awareness of my brain not working right.

I ran into the bathroom and a loud inner voice said "Devani, you HAVE to stop this right now. If you don't, you won't achieve anything that you want. Your life will be useless."

It was that exact moment that everything changed. Because this inner voice was so strong, I declared that day that I was done. That I would never touch that drug again. And I didn't.

That was a pure miracle.

Now miracles don't have to happen in such an extreme way. Small miracles can happen daily. And the more you are aware of them and feel gratitude for them, the MORE you can attract them!

I have learned how to implement this miracle mindset, which has allowed me to create a multiple 6-figure business that helps female entrepreneurs all around the world to effectively and authentically market their businesses, so they, too, can make more money and have an impact in the world.

I achieved this without ANY formal education, marketing or business background. Just *pure hustle and a miracle mindset.*

If you want to:
>> Achieve extraordinary results in your life and business
>> Wake up each day and be so lit up that this is your reality
>> Get clear on what you want
>> Release limiting beliefs so you can dream big
>> Create your own reality
>> Experience meaningful relationships

Then the next steps will be critical in you making this happen:

Cultivating a vision

To activate your miracle mindset, you need to have a vision of where you want to go. Miracles *appear when we are clear on what we want.*

You may be thinking, *well I don't know exactly what I want.*

Perhaps you are just trying to figure out your purpose and what that looks like? Great, this exercise will help with that.

When I was 6 years into my career as a hairstylist, I became bored. I started to have an urge to do something else.

I had no idea what that was. But I knew being a hairstylist was not my purpose. I had a vision of myself making more money, traveling, and experiencing the world. I wanted to feel free and be significant.

Again, I didn't know how this looked, but I felt it. This feeling is what cultivating a vision is. It's getting in tune with the core feelings of what you desire. These feelings will help lead you to experiencing miracles to allow you to achieve what you want.

Shortly after I cultivated my vision, I manifested a job opportunity in the legal industry. That job led me to meeting the woman that got me a job at a large marketing agency, which was the catalyst for getting me into the marketing space, and eventually launching my own agency.

The following questions below will help you gain clarity on your vision so you can cultivate what you desire. You don't need to know how this will happen. This is your opportunity to daydream.

The difference between vision and goals is that vision is cultivating your imagination, which is a secret to success. Goals are the action steps you need to break down to make your vision a reality. The stronger your imagination, the more you will achieve.

You just need to answer the following questions in a journal:

>> In 5 words or more, how do you want to feel when you wake up each day?
>> How do people feel when they are around you?
>> How do I feel about my career?
>> How do I feel about my family?
>> What activities are you doing when you feel inspired?
>> What are the top 3 accomplishments you want in your business?
>> What are the top 3 accomplishments you want in your life?

Manifesting for success

Now that you have answered the above questions, let's make them a reality.

How do we do that? By first *asking for what we want* and then *asking for help*. The key that most people miss is asking.
Think about it. When is the last time you actually asked for what you wanted?

Most of the time, we don't ask for help or state our desires until we are in a crisis. Then it's usually like, oh God please help me.

Or perhaps you are someone that focuses all of your energy on what you don't want, versus what you DO want?

The trick is to always be asking for what you do want.
What I am about to teach you is how to ask in a way that actually allows you to achieve it.

This strategy works like crazy.

Keep in mind that you have to be realistic. Meaning you can't ask for ten million dollars tomorrow or to magically lose 30 pounds in five days.

This also doesn't work unless you pair action with asking, which we will talk about in a minute. You can't just sit back and wait for it to fall into your lap. There's work involved.

Now that you understand some of the ground rules, here is what you do:

Grab your journal again. Make sure it's one that expresses your style. You know, it makes you smile every time you see it. Maybe one with a great quote or image.

Now I want you to write out the answers you wrote down in step one, BUT *you are going to write it out as if it has already happened*.

This is where you put your imagination hat on and write as if you are writing a story about how your life is right now.

Here is an example:

> *I am so blessed that this is my life. I wake up every single day feeling happy and loved. I live in a marvelous, light, and bright home. I dance around my beautiful big kitchen and move to the beat of the morning music as I hydrate my body and make my morning tea. I feel in flow. I feel inspired. I feel energized.*
>
> *I then sit at my quiet space in the home where I start my day with setting intentions, journaling, and meditation before slipping on my shoes to head to the*

gym to eagerly move my body. I feel healthy, strong, and sexy.

My business provides me freedom, creativity, the ability to make an impact in the world, and an income I could have never imagined! I operate a company that provides love, connection, acceptance, and support for women in business to get visible online, develop a success mindset, and breakthrough limiting beliefs. My online audience and followers are incredible! They support me and spread my message far and wide so I can help more people.
I have an incredible team of employees who I inspire and support. They surround me with amazing energy and this fuels us for success. I feel authentic, supported, inspired, committed, focused, strong, and powerful.

I have the right coaches, mentors, and support in my life that get me to where I want to be. Because of this support, there is never a challenge or problem that I can't solve. I am emotionally intelligent and able to see what is blocking me so I can move past it quickly and effectively.

Thank you for this amazing life.

Love,
Me

So as you can read above, you really can't tell if I am writing about what is actually my reality and what I want to create as my new reality. This strategy is super powerful. You can apply this to your life as a whole like I've done or use it for a particular area in your life.

I first used this strategy when I was in my twenties and was trying to get hired at a high reputation company with literally no experience.

I journaled every day about the gratitude of already having that job, even though I wasn't even hired yet. I felt the emotion of what it would be like.

In addition to this manifesting strategy, I paired it with committed action, which brings me to the next key in creating a miracle mindset.

Take committed action

Action breeds results. If you want make your dreams a reality, you have to take action. Easier said than done, right?

What holds us back from taking action? Fear.
This fear usually comes up as resistance. Whenever we are doing something new, we are leaving our comfort zone.

Resistance often shows up as procrastination, self-doubt, lack of confidence, and/or overwhelm.

Take a moment right now to look at where this is showing up in your life. Write down what comes to mind. What are the thoughts that you tell yourself?

The first step to push resistance aside and take committed action is to be clear on what it is that you want and WHY.

In the previous exercise, you got clear about what you want. Now, you're going to find that deep inner why. Why do you really want to achieve this vision? What is your selfish reason?

Those two questions are powerful. Turn the answers into statements and reflect on them when you feel resistance.

The difference between who you are and who you want to be is what you do.

When you get into a state of action, it creates momentum and a flow of energy. *The hardest part is just getting started.*

Back to my story of when I was in my twenties and working to manifest a position at the high reputation company, I used my manifesting strategy, but paired it with action by being extremely persistent. That persistent action got me the position!

Experience gratitude every day

One of the easiest ways to tap into your miracle mindset is by having gratitude daily. Recent studies show that gratitude actually improves your physical and psychological health. You sleep better, your self-esteem increases, and stress decreases.

So how can you add gratitude into your everyday life? Start waking up each day and writing out five things you are grateful for. The first one could just be that you are grateful that you even woke up! At night, write out five things that happened that day that you are grateful for.

During the day, pick out things that you are experiencing and see them in the light of gratitude. These could be simple things like the delicious cup of coffee in the morning to the dishes you get to wash.

I know. I know. Sounds crazy, right?! But if you think about it, the fact that you have dishes, food to eat off of them, and clean, running water to wash them with is easily three things on your list right there! Not to mention the ability your body has to do that task, or a dishwasher to put them into!

Just a few months ago, I was sitting in traffic, frustrated as most of us are. I quickly caught myself in this frustrated moment. I took a deep breath and changed my thinking in that moment to realizing what a blessing it was for me to even have a car and be alive and well to drive.

It's all about perception.

So how can you shift your perception to gratitude? Start making your lists morning and night. Set a calendar reminder to pop up in the middle of the day that says "I am so grateful for _____." These little reminders and routine will help you to strengthen your gratitude muscle.

When you are in a state of gratitude, you will attract more things to be grateful for. You'll stress less and you'll start to create a life by design.

Change your morning, change your life

The key to empower your life and change your life is how you start your day. The first hour of your day sets the foundation for this shift to happen.

When you look at some of the most successful CEOs in the world (Steve Jobs, Tony Robbins, and Benjamin Franklin, just to name a few) they all have one thing in common.

They wake up early and have a very disciplined morning routine. When you think about discipline and routines, you may be thinking that sounds restrictive or boring. But discipline and routines actually creates more freedom in your life!

In addition, a morning routine can actually be really fun and inspiring because you will start to see the ripple effect from committing to this routine. Here is what a typical morning routine looks like for me:

>> Wake at 6 a.m.
>> Drink a warm cup of lemon water
>> Journal for 5 minutes
>> Meditate for 10 minutes
>> Visualization for 3 minutes
>> Coffee or tea + a nutritious breakfast
>> Gym

What is great about this is that I know exactly what I am doing from the moment that I wake up. I have a plan and I start accomplishing that immediately, which puts me in the vibration of feeling accomplished and in action.

Keep in mind I was NOT a morning person. You may not be an early riser, but think about waking up just 15 minutes earlier than you normally do to get so much more done. To feel accomplished and in action right from the start. You are also getting your brain into a state of gratitude and kicking in your miracle mindset.

I remember when I first launched my company over 5 years ago. I would wake up immediately feeling overwhelmed and stressed. I had no consistency or focus in how I started my day.

Now, I start my morning calm, peaceful, inspired, and excited. I'm energized with my morning routine which feeds by body, spirit, and mind.

By default, my business has doubled every single year. I am attracting people into my life who are reflecting this peaceful aura back to me, and each area of my life has been positively impacted because of this simple routine.

One of my favorite resources for creating your own morning routine is called The Miracle Morning by my friend, Hal Elrod!

Find Your Tribe

The last (but not least!) key to achieving a miracle mindset is your tribe. What is a tribe? Commonly I refer to a tribe as a community of like-minded individuals.

I would not be where I am at today, with a successful company, meaningful relationships, and support in all areas of my life, without my tribes.

Tribes keep you connected, inspired, and focused.

We CANNOT get to where we want alone. I love the quote: "If you want to go fast, go alone. If you want to go far, bring others along." (Author unknown).

I say tribes because I have several for different areas of my life. Let me explain.

The Change[11]

In business, I have a tribe of women that I lead. They are in my online community and I influence and support them in growing their businesses.

I also have a tribe of business colleagues. These are other entrepreneurs that are at a similar level to me and we support each other in our businesses. We give feedback and collaborate with each other. This is also where I am supported by a mentor. Someone who shows me what I can't see. They give expertise and another perspective to help me make the right moves in business or life.

In life, I have my tribe of people who have similar fitness goals. I am able to be held accountable, support others, and bond in a common interest.

We live in a world where we are meant to be connected to others.

What is amazing about living in the world right now is that finding a tribe is easier than ever with the power of social media.

Two of my favorite tools for seeking out a tribe are Facebook and Meetup.com. On Facebook, if you go to Facebook.com/groups, you'll find all sorts of categories to find like-minded people. You can request to join the group, introduce yourself, and start conversations immediately.

Meetup.com is also an amazing resource, as it is designed to help you meet people in-person, as opposed to an online community. You can find a moms' group or writing club, or a group of people who are interested in literally just about anything you can think of.

To start putting this in action, commit right now to go to one new social event in the next 30 days. Even if you are going by yourself (I used to do this), your life will start to expand.

Every day for the next 30 days, spend five minutes a day posting in a relevant Facebook group. Be helpful and humble. Be open for connections and reach out to people who seem like-minded.

I have met some of the best friends in my life today from Facebook. I did this exact strategy, so you can absolutely trust that it works.

In summary, if you want to experience a miracle mindset, create a vision that lights you up from the inside out.

Take committed action on what you desire.

Be aware of your thoughts and resistance so you can crush any self-sabotage.

Feel gratitude in the little moments every day.

Discipline creates freedom.

Connection is key for achieving your greatness.

Life is NOW.

***

To contact Devani:

DevaniFreeman.com

Devani@DevaniFreeman.com

David Grossman

David Grossman, ABC, APR Fellow PRSA, helps leaders drive productivity and get the results they want through authentic leadership and communication. He's a sought-after speaker and advisor to Fortune 500 leaders, with clients including Astellas, Eastman Chemical, Health Quest, Hill-Rom, J&J, Kimberly-Clark, Lockheed Martin, McDonald's, and Tenneco, among others. David is also a three-time author. His newest award-winning book, *"No Cape Needed: The Simplest, Smartest, Fastest Steps To Improve How You Communicate By Leaps and Bounds,"* was published in the fall of 2015.

David counsels leaders at top organizations to unleash the power of strategic internal communication and drive performance. He is founder/CEO of The Grossman Group, an award-winning Chicago-based strategic leadership development and internal communications consultancy, and he teaches at Columbia University, New York City.

How Better Communication Can Improve Your Life: The Top 10 Must-Dos

By David Grossman

Effective communication remains one of the secrets to business success, and overall contentment in life. So many of the problems I see in my executive coaching and consulting work stem from communication issues. These issues derail relationships, make goals harder to achieve, limit advancement opportunities, and impede overall business success.

Leaders might think that they're communicating effectively, but research with employees from a variety of sources tells a different story. Employees don't trust the very leaders who are running global organizations today. They're skeptical and confused about their role and how they fit in. While they value and like their supervisors, many employees don't have the information they need to do their jobs well. Consequently, they're neutral or, worse yet, disengaged.

Here's what many leaders don't realize: they're already communicating whether they intend to or not. It's human nature for others to read into a leader's actions based on their own perceptions. So if we're communicating with or without intention, my thought for every leader everywhere is to get good at it.

Recently, at The Grossman Group, the strategic communications firm I founded 16 years ago, we saw a client of ours get good at it, and he's starting to see the results.

This client runs a small business, a chain of restaurants. Recently, he wanted to revitalize his leadership style to drive business results. He went through some personal leadership training, and then came to us with some ambitious goals. He hoped to shift the strategic vision from just making great food to something much more fundamental: providing employees and guests the best possible experience every time they walk in the door. Essentially, he wanted to make everyone feel great.

My client realized that goal had to start with great communication. As a leader, he had to explain through a variety of tools why the restaurant chain was in business, and what their core vision and values truly were. He also had to communicate his vision more powerfully. To bring his team along, he became more direct, stopped shying away from tough conversations, asked better questions, and engaged employees and customers more.

While the business is just beginning its journey, the work has already transformed the company's vision and strategy, and helped its leader see what truly matters.

We see this experience all the time—digging in deep to discover the right vision can reveal a much more inspiring path for clients, and for employees and customers.

Done well, communicating effectively gives you tremendous power to transform your company and your team, not to mention your relationships and your life.

Communication is a way to make a significant difference—for yourself and others. At its simplest, you can use communication to make things easier and more effective and efficient. You can also use communication to make others feel good about their jobs, to be engaged and excited, to help someone who's having a hard time get through a rough patch, or to inspire a team moving through changes or difficult times.

I've seen clients—as well as friends—use communication for high impact by coaching and mentoring someone, by influencing others who may be tentative or uncomfortable in a new role, or by helping develop a young person to be his or her best self.

In the same way, everyone can use communication, whether in business or in their personal lives. You can use it to prevent the skeptics and naysayers from spiraling into a negative pattern, or help a struggling individual find the courage and the map to make real change. And for the business leaders among us, you can use it to make substantial changes that don't just help a company or team go from "good to great" but also create a new, lasting legacy, one that is truly inspired.

That's why I believe that communication is really a superpower in today's world, and certainly in today's business and financial environment.

Based on our experiences with clients, here are what I believe to be the most important communication strategies for improving your work, and your life:

1. Really Know Your Audience

One of the most common mistakes people make is to communicate from their perspective. Sure, it makes sense that you would first approach any communication from your point of view. The trick is learning how to get beyond the assumption that everyone else shares your perspective and will perceive issues the same way you do.

It's important to remember that people act to support their best interests, so we first need to understand where they're coming from:

What do they already know about the topic?

What are their concerns?

What might they want to know?

What do I want my audience to think/feel/do?

The more you know about your audience, the better you'll be able to speak to them in a way that is meaningful for them, and influence them and move them to action.

There Are Eight Key Questions Every Employee Has

These days, employees are bombarded with so much information that it's hard for them to digest it all. Just because you say something doesn't mean others hear and understand you. And that's the whole point of communication—to create shared understanding and drive people to action.

Whether employees ask them or not, the reality is there are several key questions that are on their minds, what I call The Eight Key Questions. These questions are a lot like Maslow's hierarchy of needs, which states that people need to fulfill certain basic needs before they can move to more complex levels of thought, such as self-awareness and understanding of others. In other words, employees' basic needs—the "me-focused" needs—have to be addressed first before employees start thinking beyond themselves.

Once employees feel taken care of, they become more aware of changes or initiatives happening outside their department or function and ask the question, "What's going on?" This is a transitional question that takes employees from "me" to "we." The "we-focused" questions that follow are really about the larger organization.

The ultimate payoff is when employees ask "How can I help?" This is an expression of engagement—a willingness to do more—which also demonstrates a strong emotional connection to the organization.

INSERT 8 KEY QUESTIONS IMAGE HERE

2. Be more planful and purposeful

Being more purposeful in your communications can take as little as five minutes. I call it **"Take 5"** to communicate well. The process involves following five simple steps that can lead to better communication. With time, you can get so good at answering these questions that you can work through this on the back of a napkin. Most importantly, the messages you eventually deliver to your audiences will be better thought out and tied to the business outcomes you seek.

The Take 5 steps in a nutshell:

Outcome—What do you want to accomplish at the highest level? What's the business outcome you seek? Define it as specifically as you can.

Audience—Who's the audience? Where are they coming from? What do you want them to think, feel, and do?

Messages—Given the key audience's mindset, what are the two or three messages to move them to action?

Tactics—Is the message best delivered face-to-face, one-on-one, through email, or in another way? Consider the limitations and possible impact of each option. Important and sensitive topics deserve face-to-face communication, or at least voice-to-voice communication.

Measurement—How do you evaluate how well your message is being received? One way is to analyze the questions employees ask. If they are forward looking and asking how a new situation might work, your message is getting through. If they are challenging your assumptions or want to take a step back, you could do a better job communicating.

3. Select the right method for communicating

Just as there are specific criteria when selecting the best transportation to take on vacation, there are certain factors to consider when selecting the most appropriate communication vehicle for your message.

Keeping in mind your audience, the type of information, and how much of it you need to communicate will help you choose the right vehicle and substantially increase the likelihood that your message will be received, understood, and acted on.

Some tips for choosing the best communication channel:

Use face-to-face communication when you want to:

Address topics that require immediate action

Discuss complex, confidential, or sensitive topics or issues

Gather immediate feedback and input

Use email when you want to:

Provide directional, important, and timely information to targeted audiences

Direct the receiver to a website or online source for more information

Share detailed information and data

Use written methods of communication (letter, memo) when you want to:

Share detailed information

Provide a paper reference

Reach audiences with limited access to technology

Use the phone when you want to:

Ask questions and gather immediate feedback and input

Provide instructions or to walk someone through a process

Alert someone of a message they need to receive quickly

Share high-level or detailed news/updates

Use voicemail when you want to:

Communicate urgent, brief messages that require quick action but don't require proof that the communication was made

Request a same-day or next-day response

Communicate with team members who are traveling

Conduct a webcast (video or web presentation) when you want to:

Deliver a message to a large and geographically scattered audience in real time

Provide information and training on specific programs/initiatives

Allow for questions and answers among a group

Post information on the intranet when you want to:

Generate discussion / brainstorms among colleagues

Raise awareness and post reminders

4. Hone your messages

Ask any journalist and they can tell you about the 5 W's and an H. Any solid news story covers those six basic ingredients. The same is true for communicating with others.

Want to ensure you don't forget a critical detail in your communications? Think 5 W's and an H to ensure you're not missing an important detail, sharing the all-important context, and making it relevant for your audience.

What: What's the decision? What does it mean? What should I know? What's in it for me?

Why: Why is it the right decision? Why now? Why is it important?

Where: Where is this decision coming from? Where/what locations will it affect? Where can I get more information?

When: When is this happening?

How: How was the decision made? How will it be implemented? How will communications flow internally and externally? How does it impact me?

Who: Who made the decision? Who's in charge? Who does it impact?

In communicating your message, the order is important. Adult learners want to know the "what" first and then the "why." The rest can follow logically.

5. Provide the big-picture and context first; check for understanding before sharing more detailed information

Without context, there's no meaning.

Every employee comes into the workplace with his or her own context. It's a mix of our upbringing, culture, religion, memories, and experiences, along with our other cues and clues from the individual communicating the message. Context influences how we interpret information. It's the glasses through which we look at and understand the world.

Always begin communication with chapter one. It's "once upon a time" in headline form, and it starts at the very beginning of the story you're trying to tell. Set up the situation and show the big picture so everyone starts with the same base of knowledge. Chances are, we might be on chapter five of the story, but need to remember that others are on an earlier chapter, or need us to start at the very beginning.

As you think about how to set context, below are some of the categories to consider. Ask yourself…to understand what's happening and why, does your team need information on:

Background/history

Assumptions

Strategy and objectives

Reasons behind decisions

Roles

Relative priority

Knowledge of the stakes

Metrics/success

Remember: go slow to go fast. Providing the right insights and making them relevant to your outcome upfront will help your team make sound decisions and avoid false starts and re-work. When mistakes happen, ask yourself, "What context did I fail to set?"

6. Ask broad open-ended questions to create dialogue

One sure way to fuel conversations is with open-ended questions. Open-ended questions encourage others to express their opinions and ideas. Really listening to what others have to say shows interest and respect for their input, and simply shows that you care. The impact can be significant.

Try these open-ended questions in your next presentation or conversation:

What's your reaction to what I just said?

What's your feedback on the choices I just presented?

What are your thoughts?

Would you tell me more about …?

Can you help me understand that a little better?

How do you see this happening?

What kind of challenges are you facing?

What's the most important priority to you with this? Why?

What other issues are important to you?

What is it that you'd like to see accomplished?

7. Listen, and listen some more

During a trip to the local bookstore with my 6-year-old daughter, Avi, we sat down for a storytelling session in the children's section.

The facilitator, looking like a giant on a pint-sized blue chair, began with a simple question: "What do we need to do to get started, kids?"

The preschoolers and kindergarteners seated in a semi-circle responded in unison. "Open our ears, close our mouths, eyes on me (the facilitator)." I thought to myself, "Holy cow! That can work for leaders, too."

Here are some tried-and-true ways to become a better listener:

Approach each dialogue with the goal to learn something. Think of the person as someone who can teach you.

Stop talking and focus closely on the speaker. Suppress the urge to think about what you're going to say next or multitask.

Drill down to the details by asking directive, specific questions that focus the conversation, such as "Tell me more about..." "How did you come to this conclusion?" or "How would this work?"

Summarize what you hear and ask questions to check your understanding, such as "If I'm understanding you..." or "Tell me if this is what you're saying...."

Encourage with positive feedback. If you can see that a speaker has some trouble expressing a point or lacks confidence, encourage him or her with a smile, a nod, or a positive question to show your interest.

Listen for total meaning. Understand that in addition to what is being said, the real message may be non-verbal or emotional. Checking body language is one way to seek true understanding.

Pay attention to your responses. Remember that the way you respond to a question also is part of the dialogue. Keep an open mind and show respect for the other person's point of view, even if you disagree with it.

Ensure shared understanding/meaning before the conversation ends

8. When appropriate, empathize and reflect back feelings

Empathy in the workplace involves understanding how others feel and imagining what it's like to be in someone else's shoes.

Listening empathetically lets your employees know you care because it taps one of our strongest human drives—to be heard and understood. You don't have to agree with how someone else feels. In fact, your reaction might be the exact opposite. But empathy inherently isn't about you—it's about the other person. Listen fully and play back how someone else feels.

Here are five critical steps to demonstrate empathy and better connect with your employees:

1) Listen without interruption, and focus solely on the other person.

2) Pause and imagine how your employee is feeling.

3) Show you hear them by reflecting back what they are saying: "What I hear you saying is…"

4) Validate their feelings: "I understand you're feeling…"

5) Support and close the conversation.

The payoff from showing empathy is an employee who knows you care, which is motivating. At the same time, you gather information that's useful for you.

9. Have calmer and more courageous conversations

I firmly believe that we have more courage inside each of us than we may think, and that it's powerful to tap some of that—for our benefit and the benefit of others. This means we need to have more tough conversations. Many of us have important things that remain unsaid, and addressing issues upfront is the only way to keep everyday speed bumps from mushrooming into larger problems.

When you do have these tough conversations, start with sharing your motivation and intent.

Tell people what they need to hear—not what they want to hear. It's often through tough conversations that we build relationships and cement bonds. These courageous conversations should also include asking for what you need to succeed. When a deadline is unrealistic, do you ask for time to do quality work? When you're missing background information for a project, do you politely insist on a briefing before you begin work? It might be easier to remain silent, but being assertive shows that you respect yourself and others.

10. Look in the mirror

After you communicate, spend a few minutes to look in your own mirror to reflect on how you did and assess whether you had the impact you wanted.

Ask yourself:

Did I take the time to plan my communications?

Was I prepared in delivering my message?

Did I listen more than I talked?

Was there productive dialogue?

Did I check for understanding?

Did I get the reaction I wanted?

Am I seeing a change in the person's (or people's) actions?

Conclude by asking yourself what might you do differently to be even more successful if you have the chance to communicate again? What can you learn from what happened, and how can you apply that in the future?

Close

Communication—done well—can be tough. To get good at anything—whether in sports, business, or my latest focus, parenting—you need to work at it. Experts in anything practice. As long as you keep working on the skill, you can transform the way you communicate—and you'll be a stronger, more respected leader because of it. You might even say you've discovered your own superpower—and there's no cape needed.

***

To Contact David:

dgrossman@yourthoughtpartner.com | 312-850-8200

Book David to Speak: www.yourthoughtpartner.com/speaking-and-events

Get David's Books: www.yourthoughtpartner.com/book

Subscribe to David's Blog: http://www.yourthoughtpartner.com/blog

Subscribe to the eNewsletter: http://www.yourthoughtpartner.com/ethought-starters

Connect on LinkedIn: https://www.linkedin.com/in/davidgrossmanaprabc

Follow on Twitter: www.twitter.com/ThoughtPartner

Kelli Locatelli

Kelli Locatelli is an entrepreneur and seasoned self-starter with dedication, drive, passion and exceptional leadership skills. Building lifelong relationships is of utmost importance to her.

At the age of 19, Kelli became the CEO of a software company, which led to a successful career in Executive Sales and Marketing, managing high-profile public figures. Recognizing the need for technology convergence in the entertainment industry connecting musicians and athletes, creating a channel market combining the two worlds together, she developed her promotion company.

Kelli has won numerous awards in Sales and Marketing as well as being acknowledged as a Forbes Top 500 Social Media Experts and Influential Women in Business. Kelli is an Inspirational Speaker. Certified Life Coach, Certified Interventionist, and Mentor/Coach in Personal Development. She teaches the essence of "Sur-Thriving".

When you ask anyone connected with Kelli, they will tell you there is a sense of ease about her, whether it be her sense of humor, honesty, or ability to interact with people of all walks of life. She believes integrity and trust have been the thread to all her many successes. She applies compassion and gratitude towards family, life, and business.

LIFE: What I Signed Up For
By Kelli Locatelli

She laid in the back of the car in absolute fear. The doctors were called ahead of time. Unsure what to expect, they knew it had taken some time to get her there and that it was an emergency situation. On December 22, 1968, my mom, pregnant with me, had the Hong Kong flu. With just a cough, her placenta had erupted and separated from her uterus. She didn't know what had happened; she just knew something wasn't right. She shared this frightening story with me, with a look only a mother could give that said, "I did what I had to do." The strength she showed is so clear to me, today, as I know exactly why I came full circle to find myself in the emergency room at 46 fighting for my life again as I received well over 700 stitches.

As they were preparing her for an emergency C-section, she noticed the look on the faces of her doctor and pediatrician. All she could do was scream in fear to get the baby out. Whatever they had given her for the surgery didn't take effect and she felt the cold blade against her belly, she could hear the doctors and the concern in their voices, "Oh my God, look at all that blood"! It was truly life or death for both of us. I was drowning in blood and she was starting to see colors fading in and out. She heard, "It's a girl" and her mind took her somewhere else, no doubt trying to protect her from the pain of the surgery, as they worked.

All I knew growing up was what she had always said to me, "You were born a fighter!" *Born a fighter*. I didn't know what this meant yet, I just knew that I was born to make a difference. That I would fight for myself, and I would stand up for others, knowing they needed me. I somehow knew I was different. There was a sense of *"not quite fitting in,"* and yet still being a part of the *"cool kids"* throughout my life.

I worked at a very young age, fostering the entrepreneurial spirit as I know it today. My parents divorced and the *"do whatever it takes"* attitude took hold of me. I was nineteen when I got my first big break, running a start-up company. I was later recruited into larger corporations in Silicon Valley, which led me to my final corporate job in the dot-com arena. I had found a place of belonging, an important position, working with high-profile people from entertainment to technology convergence. I am so grateful for the people I met, and all I learned during my corporate years. Sales and marketing prepared me well for my future endeavors. Then the dot-com bubble of mad money burst. I was divorced at this point with two small children and decided to start my own company. This is when I met my second husband.

It was just after Christmas 2004 and we were planning on spending New Year's with our friends at Pismo Beach riding quads and having a blast. I had very little experience with 4 wheelers. Yet having been active my entire life, I never had an issue with fear and I was excited to learn and do a bit of showing off. After practicing on the beach, riding up and down the gorgeous coastline of Central California, I was ready to hit the dunes! As I followed him, I tried to keep up my speed since he was much more experienced than I was. Going down a sand bowl and realizing I was going way too fast, I panicked. There was no one around me. I hit the clutch, breaks, accelerator, and locked the front wheels. It was in complete slow motion that I began to dive over the front of this 600lb quad. I thought to myself, "Oh God, please don't let it land on my back." Years earlier, I was diagnosed with degenerative disc disease and had several problems throughout my back. As I landed in the sand with the quad landing on me and burying me in the sand, prayers were answered as it didn't land on my back—however, it landed on my neck and thorax. The bike was thrown off me, which had knocked me unconscious, though I had no idea. I didn't go to the hospital. In fact, I did nothing except prepare for some bruises and with the adrenaline was actually quite angry, feeling as though I had somehow ruined our trip.

It took eleven months before the pain began to render my arms completely useless. I remember screaming in pain to just cut my

The Change[11]

arms off. It felt like fire going through my veins and around my shoulders, and nothing helped. At this point, I was on morphine and it may as well have been candy because it didn't relieve anything. My kids were little and I was scared. Finally, I met with a spinal orthopedic surgeon, who was shocked to see I had cracked two vertebrae in my neck. I will never forget what he said to me—"I have no idea how you are alive, but you are. There is no explanation how you are walking around and not paralyzed"! Then he said to me, "Kelli, you should be in a wheelchair, like Christopher Reeve, but without the breathing tubes. Your silver lining is not just silver—it's bedazzled." This was the funniest thing I had ever heard, a bedazzled silver lining! He knew he could joke with me, he understood I found the humor in the situation, and scheduled me for surgery.

I was told I wouldn't be able to speak for 2 weeks, which I knew would scare my kids. I was told I would be on medication for the rest of my life and if I'm lucky, with nuts, bolts, and plates in my neck and someone else's bones replacing mine that I might regain 20% movement. I spoke the same day as the surgery when I saw my family. I knew I had a long road ahead, I just wasn't very worried about it. I figured, *hey I'm here, let's do what we can and get through it!* A few weeks later, I received a text message from my husband… reading, *"This is not what I signed up for"* and he moved to Texas. My 18-month recovery period was cut down to get up and get it together. I relied on my mom again during this period. I also relied on the pain pills, the anxiety pills, and the muscle relaxers. I had no idea of the addictive power of narcotics. No one told me my body and my mind had two different agendas with these medications. No one warned me of the ridiculous addictive hold they could have. And I realized I felt nothing at all.

As I sat in my pain management doctor's office, I told him I wanted to get off these medications. He assured me we would cut them back a little at a time and it would be simple. In fact, he commended me on wanting to get off them, as he prescribed a stronger medication. I felt mentally strong and never was I afraid of this change. It was a crazy and dangerous cocktail which I was fully functional on, or so I thought. Here we go—my mom was there to help me through one of the bravest things I thought I would ever do. I zipped the five different narcotics up into a quart size baggie, the muscle relaxers, the anxiety pills, the patches, and had my brother pick up my kids. I told my mom to hang on because this would not be like the movies, and it wasn't. It was *horrifying*. I went cold turkey off all these medications at one time and was going to fight through this too. I'm not an addict, I did not choose this, yet here I was getting ready for the unexpected. Through the night, the withdrawal got worse and worse. I felt like I wanted to crawl out of my own skin—it itched, I was shaking, throwing up and weak, yet wide awake and began to hallucinate. My mom had called my doctor and based on a "point system" of withdrawal, everything was "normal." It's normal to see shadows, to hear circus animals and circus songs? To hear dogs that are not there barking and to be so weak I couldn't lift my body, nor control any of its functions?

My mom lay beside me, calm on the outside, sick on the inside. I kept asking if it was time to go to the doctor, who was to give me the antidote which was going to close the synapses firing off in my brain, causing these physical reactions I was experiencing to stop immediately. It was more than just the hope this would work that pulled me through. I now have learned the strength of tapping into our brains to get through such events. At the time, I did not understand what I was doing for myself. Yet when we look back, isn't it a wonderful experience to know we truly had the power at every moment in life?

I began to hear things and see things and asked my mother if she did too. She would listen and lay her head back down, so I would too. Not being able to dress myself or walk as the morning came, I scooted down the stairs and really don't remember how I got into the back of the car as she drove me to the doctor. I do remember singing and making my mom laugh, to comfort us both that relief was on the way and this would soon be over! He was supposed to be ready for me. I couldn't see because my eyes were so dilated. I was so sick, scared, and just tired of this horrific feeling with jumpiness and paranoia that had taken me over. He finally gave my mom a prescription to go get filled, as I waited. I laid there and begged for relief. I was rattling inside my body and the next thing I knew, I woke up in the emergency room to see my brother and mom whispering to each other. I remember the fear in their eyes, as they met the fear in mine. I had seized twice, bit through my tongue, and was revived in the E.R. *A fighter, I had made it.*

I was so angry that I was told I had to be on medication for the rest of my life, angry that I believed them. I realized and decided I had a choice. I had always known with a plan I could set my goals and mind to achieve anything. I knew I had to dig deep and find courage. I noticed complete strangers drifting, not living, without any certainty in their lives. I began to research these drugs and this so-called addiction. I then began to speak at pain management seminars and shared my story with authorized dealers. I made it clear it was not OK what I had gone through and it is beyond difficult to wean off such powerful drugs. I certainly do not suggest going cold turkey as I did, yet we have to educate one another about this *epidemic*. I use the word epidemic broadly because once I was clear of mind, I knew I had the power, and I got to choose.

Have you looked around lately and noticed so many people are wandering around in life, and choosing to not choose? Whether it's the noise that surrounds us daily, or the need to be "busy" creating a lack of happiness. I became a mentor not just because of my life battle lessons, but rather to prevent such extreme lessons with others. Look around at all the heads looking down, as you're looking up. Anything can be a drug if you allow it, and nothing is addicting once you have the tools to decide for yourself. This is how powerful our minds truly are.

A few years later, a night of absolute darkness fell upon me and my kids. We had gone to a wedding, one which none of us really wanted to attend but felt a strange obligation. I can only say my memory of this night is not clear. My son and I had a fight, and my daughter was in my back seat as we left the wedding. My tire blew on the freeway and life in my mind was over. Nothing was in alignment. It was the darkest time in my life that would show up in ways I could never have anticipated. The lessons the universe sent would soon be my breakthrough.

The first of these came in the form of another tire blow out. This time I was in a rental car. I was supposed to pick up my new car that morning and was on time for an appointment out of town. I called my rep at the dealership and told him I would stop by after my appointment, knowing when you are buying a new car, it never really goes as smooth as "sign here, sign there"! The rental car I was given was ridiculous for the area I was living. As I headed out, I heard what sounded like a gunshot, and the car was out of control. The driver's side tire had blown. There was a mountain on my left and a lake on my right. It wasn't until I skidding 100 feet into a half frozen lake that I saw the road I was driving on. I remember the car being out of control and spinning, though I didn't know I had rolled up the mountain, pushing me onto the bank of the lake, half on the road, half on the icy rocks. I immediately unlocked the seat belt, which thrashed me forward into the steering wheel. I screamed as if anyone could hear me. I saw the water filling up through the sides of the car. Not understanding by the time the car hit the bottom of the algae lake, the cold water would have sent me into shock, just as it had *two people two days prior* as they fell to their death the exact same way.

As the water got closer to my chest, I recall my hand in my hair pulling it, thinking I'm not getting out of here. The water was not cold. It didn't scare me. In fact, it's said your life flashes before your eyes in this type of situation and mine did not. My future showed itself to me in a clear vision. I felt courageous and I pulled, kicked, desperately looking for a way to escape. I saw my daughter getting married, my son and his kids, I saw them graduating from college and I began to bang on the automatic window tabs, so silly because the hood of the car was in my face, the entire car was almost submerged in the water, then the driver side window, and only the

The Change[11]

driver side window went down, disappeared. I crawled out feet first, and in my humor again, having just recently bought a Michael Kors purse which floated up to me as I'm waving to the people on the bank, I grabbed my purse. I couldn't hear what they were yelling as I was hanging on to the roof of the car. I just began to swim, purse on my head, ducking under chunks of ice. I didn't see the freeway was completely shut down; I didn't notice anything until they pulled me from the frozen water.

What happened next was extremely weird, at the time. I saw the hood of the car go under water and I felt I was in it. What started as me joking around with the two men that pulled me out turned into a question—had I just died in that car? I didn't believe they could see me. I felt as though I wasn't standing there. Has this ever happened to you? Unsure of reality? Later I came to accept, *I did not physically die; what passed away were all the things that no longer served me in my life!* Reflecting later, how I felt in this moment is I had gained momentum to continue learning I was not a statistic, at least not one that had to live with these events as a type of self-punishment. Have you told a story before, believing you deserved what you got? Everything I had ever done was in absolute perfect timing as I continued to learn I have the power to heal myself, mentally and physically. Through a horrible wreck in which others lost their lives, I did not. This meant something very powerful to me, and I became closer to completing this circle of awakening. The ultimate lesson was coming…

Forward to July, the same year after wrecking in the lake in January. I was packed that day and headed for California, where I had a meeting planned that evening. I noticed earlier when I had run to the store to get my waters, twigs, nuts, and berries to hold me over for the drive that I had left my door to the garage unlocked. I thought nothing of it, as I always did a triple check around my house before leaving for several days, as I would do that day. As I spoke to my friend on the phone, I started to get sleepy, and we agreed I really should take a 30-minute nap before driving seven hours. I set my alarm.

I never heard the alarm go off. I woke to a man standing in my room, I wasn't sure if I was dreaming or not. Charging at him, the result of an instinct to scare him away, I was stabbed in the chest. The force threw me back. I was tortured, and taunted, was cut several places on my neck and around it, on my wrists, arms, knees, and multiple areas all over my body. I had lost one third of my blood and though I had fought, I was in and out of consciousness and left for dead. What I remember clearly was I woke up with the feeling that *someone or something* had literally blown air into my lungs and I gasped for the air. I couldn't move. I felt wet, my arms wouldn't work, and I couldn't lift my body. I listened, hoping that the pounding of my heart was the only thing I would hear. I rolled my body back and forth to gain momentum and threw myself on the carpet. Dialing 911 with a toe, I was unaware of the severity of what had happened. Spending several days in the ICU and over 700 stitches later, I eventually again used humor to eliminate the absolute fear from what the doctors were telling me. Humor has a way of making you and others believe all is ok. My kidneys, pancreas, and liver had shut down—I was given 24 hours to live.

When I was released from the hospital, I asked my chosen little sister, who had been there for me the entire time, to take me back to my house. Bonnie, in all her love, begged me not to go, that she had already been there and did not want me to see. I won the battle, and we went into my room where I too became sick and full of panic at what I was looking at. I ran to the bathroom and could not believe what I saw. It was as if I was in a movie and yet the setting was my room, my sanctuary! Shaking and sweating, in pain and disbelief, a tremendous amount of strength and clarity overwhelmed me. Looking at Bonnie with the tears in both our eyes, without a word being said, we both knew: *I had won the fight for my life.*

My mind hit the place of ENOUGH IS ENOUGH, and words from mentors I had aligned myself with rang like bells in my head. I had learned the Power of Letting Go, and I applied it. It hit me—I had put myself in a 2% statistic my whole life and joked about it, yet the events were not funny. I used humor to make others comfortable as they learned and listen to me share my stories. People had such pity for me, yet I was embracing these lessons and I refused to be a victim. In all areas of my life, the thread of survival shared throughout my life no longer served me, so I let it go.

Have you ever gone through something, literally anything in your life, and thought it was so bad that what else could happen? Be aware of these thoughts because if you wonder what else could happen, ultimately it's going to. Now you get to decide to hang on or let go. Once I was able to take inventory of all I had been through, including the smaller events and influences, the wins and losses, I began to ask myself, *"What is the lesson in this, and how can I be grateful for it?"*

I live my life *feeling* through whatever may be facing me. This is different than *thinking* it through. When you *FEEL* through each and every situation, as I ultimately did, you begin to see things exactly as they are. It's not always easy—it is necessary! It took me a lot of courage and strength. Once you have observed yourself and your reactions to situations, you will stop reacting and begin deciding. For example, the best way for me to let go and let love was to first forgive all those that have told me I couldn't or I wouldn't, tried to take me out and did not—this allowed me to forgive myself. I had to apply this to me in order to live, learn, and teach. There is no life or death; there is only life. Let breakdowns become breakthroughs, allow past obstacles to become lessons. We are able to choose. We are allowed to change our story. Where I was just a fighter, just a survivor, I am a now a *"SUR-THRIVER."* This is my PHD, to help others become a *"BATTLE LIFE WARRIOR"*... *I learned to fight with my will to live and my heart to love.*

> *"Mommy, you are pink in a world that is gray."*—my daughter, Marley Locatelli
>
> *"My Mom is my hero, she loves me no matter what."*—my son, Tyler Locatelli

***

To Contact Kelli

Cell: 530-786-8265

Office: 916-568-9700

WWW.KELLILOCATELLI.COM

WWW.MENTORWITHKELLI.COM

https://www.facebook.com/kelliphillipslocatelli

www.facebook.com/kellilocatelli

https://www.linkedin.com/in/kellilocatelli

https://mobile.twitter.com/kellilocatelli

https://www.instagram.com/kellilocatelli/

Snapchat: Kelli Locatelli

Kasey Higbee

Author, speaker, philanthropist, and entrepreneur, Kasey Higbee says; "I wish for a life lived to the fullest potential at every turn. My desire is to use my talents and resources to positively impact as many lives as I can." This has been Kasey's mission and her purpose for the past decade and every decision she makes aligns with that vision. In fact, that is why she contributed to this very book, because she knows, *"The Change* will be a transformative tool in thousands of lives worldwide."

Helping individuals and organizations identify their deepest desires, develop strategies to accomplish those goals, and refine the process to increase efficiency and outcomes is Kasey's passion. Currently, she is one of the leading affiliates in the world's fastest growing personal development company. She is able to facilitate sudden and significant change in lives around the globe, while simultaneously growing her own lucrative international business. She is headed to the top and bringing as many people with her as possible. So, if her message resonates with you, and you are willing to bring your rock solid work ethic and enthusiasm to the table, then she is completely confident that she and her team can teach you the rest. *Let's change the world! It's go time!*

Nay-sayers be damned!

By Kasey Higbee

Columbus was not void of passion when he sailed the seas and discovered America; his enthusiasm at times was perhaps the only wind in his sails. President Lincoln was not apathetic in his pursuit to abolish slavery—thank God! Tesla did not receive patents for a system of transmitting electrical energy because he was indifferent to his project. Thomas Edison didn't invent the lightbulb in one fell swoop; it took perseverance. Martin Luther King's "I Have a Dream" speech is not remembered for being delivered in monotone. Neil Armstrong didn't become the first person to walk on the Moon as a result of half-heartedly training for his journey. Michael Jordan didn't make it from Brooklyn to the NBA without a passionate pursuit. Oprah didn't become the media proprietor, talk show host, actress, producer, and philanthropist we know today by way of disinterest in her own success. Think of your greatest accomplishments in life to date; were they achieved void of zest, vigor, and zeal? Not likely. Ralph Waldo Emerson put it simply, "Nothing great was ever achieved without enthusiasm."

We have within us Greatness—a limitless reservoir of Ultimate Potential, Power, and Purpose. You can call this greatness God or Source. You can attribute it to spirituality or science. I am not interested in that argument. A rose by any other name is still a rose. What matters is that right now, this incredible potential is percolating within you! So how do we unleash the potential, tap into that power, and live our purpose? Well, it won't happen by accident; it takes decision and action, fueled by both serious intention and enthusiasm.

Let us start by examining the enthusiasm gurus—children. Every child has grandiose dreams of being an astronaut, the president, a pop-star, or, in my brother's case, a cocker spaniel! What did you want to be when you grew up? What did you long for? When your young imagination ran wild, what adventures did you find yourself on? How many yards were you willing to mow in order to get the telescope you wanted so you could see beyond the stars? As a young child with a dream, to what lengths would you go to see that dream fulfilled? Nay-sayers be damned! To hell with the doubters, realists, and critics! A child's dream is impermeable; it is protected by their enthusiasm and faith.

Envision this: a little boy who dreams of becoming a firefighter is watching television when he hears a distant siren growing closer. He jumps to his feet, smiling from ear to ear. In less than 2.2 seconds, he crosses the living room, scales the davenport, crawls under the dining-room table, and smashes his doe-eyed face against the front window. He grins just to catch a glimpse of the fire engine as it passes by his house. *That* is enthusiasm!

Upon hearing the sirens, he didn't begin calculating the potential ROI of his efforts. He didn't think of the cost-benefit ratio or potential consequences of his actions. He heard the sirens calling to a deep passion in his soul and he went running.

This is not to say enthusiasm trumps due diligence. As mature adults with an understanding of cause and effect, we would be remiss to ignore the potential costs of our actions. But as we do so, we run the risk of dimming our passionate flame inside. We must walk this line with caution; vigilant in our efforts to fan the flame of excitement as we navigate the obstacles that line the path we have chosen to take.

As we age, our aspirations mature and develop, as does everything that grows. However, our enthusiasm for our dreams doesn't have to wane simply because our dreams change and grow. In fact, those who maintain youthful enthusiasm in pursuit of their mature dreams are the ones who cross the finish line first, and are still smiling ear-to-ear.

What happens then, as we age, that dampens our spirit and disconnects us from this Greatness, this life-giving Source within? *We change.* We relinquish control to external forces; we buy into limiting beliefs and self-destructive patterns. Like a frog brought slowly to a boil, we allow our Greatness to escape from within us, little-by-little as the surrounding world changes. We're picked last for games at recess; we don't grasp algebra as easily as our classmates; our bodies look different than those of our peers; we have no date to prom; we don't get accepted to our first choice of college; a boyfriend or girlfriend finds us lacking and we find ourselves alone; we didn't get the job, or if we did, our boss doesn't appreciate our work; bills are overdue; the house payment is behind… and life goes on, and on, and on. Therein lies mankind's greatest tragedy: we begin to weave together a tapestry of lies about who we are, what we can accomplish, and what we are worth. Under the weight of such despair, our enthusiasm retreats to protect our egos from yet another bash.

So what do I say to this? Well, with all due respect, we need to grow up. I know it is paradoxical to encourage us to maintain youthful enthusiasm while simultaneously calling upon us all to handle failure with wisdom and maturity, but your dreams depend on your doing so! Paulo Coelho's remark rings true, "There is just one thing that makes your dream become impossible: the fear of failure." This fear of failure is real for us all, to varying degrees. The issue is not that the fear exists; rather, it is how we choose to respond to this fear that makes or breaks us.

Perhaps it is a result of the increasingly dramatic nature of mankind that, by-and-large, we perceive failure as finite—a destination rather than a detour. Herein lies another opportunity to change a limiting belief and fiercely hold on to a rather liberating truth: failure is *not* an end result, but simply the result of quitting before you're done! Consider what some of the greats have said on the subject:

- "Our greatest glory is not in never falling but in rising every time we fall." - Confucius
- "I didn't fail 1,000 times. The lightbulb was an invention with 1,000 steps." - Thomas Edison
- "You never fail until you stop trying." - Albert Einstein

- "Every strike brings me closer to the next home run." - Babe Ruth
- "Success consists of going from failure to failure without loss of enthusiasm." - Winston Churchill
- "I've failed over and over again in my life. That is why I succeed." - Michael Jordan

If you're awake at all, what you begin to notice about the successful people in this world is not that they *never* fail, but that despite failing *often*, they keep pressing forward. This is not a phenomenon beyond our understanding. It is quite simple; a change in mindset can take the ordinary and propel them into extraordinary. This is true for you and me alike!

From as early as I can remember, my father taught me about choice and accountability. If fingers were pointed in our home, they were only allowed to be pointed inward. These lessons were hard at times; actually painful and confusing for a hormonal female teen like me. However, with a relentless love, my father's aim was to instill within my four brothers and me an internal locus of control. No outside circumstances, events, influences, or people could determine our fate. Nor was our life to be viewed as a result of chance or random happening. We were taught that our destiny was the result of our beliefs and subsequent choices and actions. This mindset demands personal accountability and admonishes the victim mentality. This mindset encourages endurance, self-awareness, growth, and the ongoing passionate pursuit of a life lived to the fullest. This mindset fuels success.

"Okay Kasey," you think skeptically as you search for a flaw in my logic. "If a man or woman can succeed at anything they have unlimited enthusiasm for, and they understand failure is nothing more than a stepping stone, then why aren't more people wildly successful?"

To which I reply, "It is simple; the majority of us lack an acute awareness of what we want."

Remember, the little boy from my example above, who tore through the living room to see the fire truck pass by? Had he not known that he desperately wanted to be a fireman, the siren would have still sounded and he would have heard its high pitch above his television program, but would he have gone running? No. You see, if we don't know what we want, then we won't know where to focus our enthusiasm and efforts. Being blind to your desires and dreams can lead to one of two outcomes. One, you become a drone floating through life without direction. Or, like an untied helium balloon, you erratically travel throughout space and time, exerting small bursts of energy here and there, never fully arriving anywhere, until you find yourself completely deflated.

Listen. Do you want the four points of success summed up in 14 words? Here:

- Figure out what you want.
- Get fired up about it.
- Take action.
- Don't stop.

My advice, which I hope you heed, is to *not* rush through step one. The rest will follow naturally once you have a clear, precise vision of what it is you want.

As a life coach, public speaker, author, and citizen of the world, I work with students, businessmen and women, presidents and CEOs of multimillion dollar companies, non-profit organizations, mothers, fathers, orphans, *the* elderly, the rich, and the poor. What I have found is that no one has the exact same life dream and set of desires. More importantly, I have found that no one's dreams are less valid, less worthy of pursuit, or less honorable or attainable than anyone else's. Yet when we begin an exercise of self-discovery to align ourselves with our dreams, we often look to what other people have created, strived for, or valued. You cannot foster the enthusiasm needed nor nurture the type of perseverance required to pursue someone else's dream; you *must* create your own dream. Choose to have the courage to own that dream and do what it takes to achieve it!

For many of my clients uncovering their life's passion and deepest desires is a matter of starting with their values. If you're open to the exercise, I invite you to partake: Go online and search for "list of values". As you read over the hundreds of values listed, choose your top 10 and order them from most important on down. Resist the temptation to create a list that your husband would like or your mother would be proud of; this is your list, your values, and it doesn't have to be approved by anyone but you. This part of the exercise might take five minutes, but for some I have seen this take five months. The length of time it takes is not important. The end result we seek is a genuine list of your top 10 values.

With that list set aside, envision all the things you want in life. It is easy to list the material things we'd like to possess (houses, cars, vacations), so start there if need be. However, also consider the intangibles. How do you physically feel? How about emotionally? What about your relationships? Who is in your life? How do they feel about you and you them? Shoot! How do you feel about yourself? Think about the daily stuff; what is your typical morning like? What does work mean to you? What do you do for a living? Who do you see daily? Some of my clients find it easy to get a quick paragraph or so jotted down, but get stuck when asked for more. If this is you, close your eyes and ask yourself to imagine every detail of your life if you lived each day void of any excuses.

Next, begin finding connections between that which you desire (your "wants") and that which you value (your "whys"). Knowing what you want is powerful; supporting that desire with an awareness of why you want it makes your pursuit indestructible. Keep your "wants" and your "whys" at the forefront of your mind. Like arrows of your mighty quiver, they are ready to be fired at any challenges that may arise. If your actions bring you closer to that which you want, do not retreat! Recite out loud your 10 values and push forward, knowing that you have within you Greatness; a limitless

The Change[11]

reservoir of Ultimate Potential, Power, and Purpose. Do not fear failure. Do not fear success. If you must fear, then fear only an ambivalent life where your amazing potential is left untapped.

If you come across a roadblock and you just want to give up, I am willing to bet you have not truly determined what it is you want. If you had, then your enthusiasm could propel you past the obstacle and on to success. Make the change. The change is to begin relentlessly pursuing your own life, not the lives others have designed for themselves. The change is to shift from an external to an internal locus of control. The change is to know what you want intimately, not casually. The change is to not fear failure (or success), but to embrace the journey. The change is taking place within you. The change is you. The change is now.

***

To learn more about Kasey's work:

www.wealthwithinyourreach.com

www.networkofsuccess.com

www.LinkedIn.com/In/kaseyhigbee

omnigrateful@gmail.com

Anna Horst

Anna helps individuals all over the world realize and actualize their potential as self-empowered creators of their greatest dreams by becoming 'Masters of Manifestation.' She has a vast intuitive understanding of human behavior and our creative abilities as pure, eternal awareness expressing life in physical form. Having a solid and deep experiential knowing of the most cutting-edge spiritual and quantum physics concepts, she is able to come into any situation and provide a level of awareness that enhances the individual's experience regardless of where they are along their path. Do you desire inner and outer peace, balance, health, clarity, and harmony in your life? Let's peel back the layers of conditioning, limiting beliefs, past traumas, and pain to align with your authentic core self. Let's resolve your innermost fears to increase awareness and make conscious choices which are aligned with your heart's deepest passions, which will enable you to flourish, thrive, and create the life of your dreams! Allow Anna to help you along your journey of self-realization and empowerment, holistic healing, harmonic co-creation, and alignment with the divine source within to create the life that you have, up until now, only dreamed of.

Conscious Empowerment

By Anna Horst

Each of us are immensely powerful creators who are continuously manifesting our entire life experience with every choice we make. We can create the life of our greatest dreams by being conscious of our choices, or if we're not consciously choosing, we are unconsciously creating what may feel more like a nightmare. Every feeling we maintain, thought process we engage, word we speak, and action we take breathes life into the energies we are choosing. We create our reality. This is not just some hypothetical idea that is solely meant to inspire you, nor is it a metaphorical concept. 'I create my reality' is a direct, accurate, and absolute truth which will be experientially proven to any individual who is honestly willing to shift their perspectives and choices, even just a little bit, to really reveal the truth for themselves.

Our energetic state of being is directly reflected in our physical reality. How we feel at the most fundamental, raw level now is the energy we are creating as our physical experience to come. We do not manifest by imagining what we want and desire. We manifest our greatest dreams by aligning with the feeling of already being and already having. When we are being compassionate to all, including our self, we experience physical scenarios that reflect and mirror that compassion. When we are expressing desperation, because we feel financially insecure, then our life will reflect that desperation in the circumstances that unfold.

Whether we are allowing, accepting, embracing, surrendering, and open to the vibrant flow of infinite creation with our whole being because we are embodying unconditional love for all, while knowing that all that is happening is happening for our best interest, or whether we are tense, forcing, fighting, resisting, denying, closed off to and struggling against the vibrant flow of infinite creation, because of underlying fears, determines whether we are creating our ideal life full of joy or creating more strain and pain. Struggle is direct resistance to our current experience, due to fear of lack, and only creates more struggle and then, eventually, desperation for relief. Expression of our authentic core self, which is inherently the frequency of absolute love, or resistance to that, is our personal choice and is chosen by the focus of our awareness.

Our thinking mind is a creative tool we can use to shift our manifestations, and each Now moment is where all the creation power resides. The content of our thoughts determine if we're creating the life of our dreams by focusing on what makes our heart sing, or if we are sabotaging our creative flow with thoughts based on guilt, judgment, shame, doubt, fear, and other disempowering ideas about our self and others. Are the thoughts we're entertaining flowing from unconditional love or are they distorted through the lens of fear?

What we choose to focus our awareness on is our own personal choice. Our only true responsibility is to choose our current energetic state of being and expression, as that is where the essence of our entire life flows from. Our current energetic state of being is where all the love and presence we have to offer flourishes to meet our physical reality and the others we share life with. When we are aware that we are actively choosing our own creative experience, we are authentically empowered with an internal power that can never be threatened by external means. Free will is the Creator's ultimate gift to us, along with the blessing of life itself, and can never be taken away. Personal choice of our energetic state in each moment is something we all are granted, such as the choice to be joyful and grateful for life even while amidst the most challenging of situations.

Most of us do not realize the base core energies we are emitting within each moment. Most of us are not creating consciously and therefore, are unconsciously responding to our environment and our physical circumstances. We allow the circumstances that surround us to seemingly dictate our current state of being and expression, which is, in essence, renouncing our own personal choice. We are allowing ourselves to be victims of circumstance, lack, and our own fear, instead of empowered as a conscious creator of our grandest dreams.

We live in a seemingly love-starved society where so many individuals can't even imagine what true happiness within each moment feels like, let alone manifest that as the foundation of one's experience. So many of us are looking externally for love, acceptance, validation, little bits of pleasure, to feel good and to be filled. The whole time we're searching, we cannot find the wholeness, peace, love, bliss, acceptance, and fulfillment that already exists within our own inner being, and is only accessed by complete acceptance of and by fully embracing life this very moment, the moment of Now. We cannot find because we are seeking, striving, and reaching for, in our current experience, that which we do not yet feel we have. So our base core state of being is one of lack, and lack is what our experiences will reflect from that level of creation. We are succumbing to suffering and defeat within the current moment in order to strive for a goal, accomplishment, idea of success, and reward later on.

Most of us do not realize within our current experience how desperate we really feel deep in our being, because without a contrast to the feelings of lack within, our inner pain, longings, and strife feels hauntingly normal. We will not be able to cognitively comprehend the sweet release peace brings to our exerting tension until we actually experience the internal shift ourselves. Struggle may just seem like the necessary effort to get through each day effectively, until a permeating peace flows into our experience sharing with us that even effort is unnecessary. Only when we experience the contrast of full surrender and allowance will we really understand how uptight and closed off we've been in order to make ourselves feel safe, accomplished, and secure.

We hide our deeper, genuine feelings in favor of more acceptable surface level expressions such as hard work, goals, education, family values, success, and doing what is 'decent.' We suggest to the world and ourselves that we are happy and life is going okay, but deep down we feel an underlying sense of lack, fear, and dissatisfaction in our current experience. So we strive for circumstances that will temporarily alleviate our pain within, and we work towards creating experiences we think will entail happiness and peace later on 'after our goals are accomplished.' We strive for success, fulfillment, financial security, and a sense of freedom from the struggle only because we feel less than adequate, insecure, a fear of failure, and lack of freedom now. Why would we be reaching for security and freedom if we already felt completely secure and free? Why would we painfully strive for more if it already felt absolutely amazing just as it is? We unhappily work hard now to ensure we get what we deserve in the future, constantly striving for the sense of freedom we may feel while sitting on a beach somewhere with no cares in the world. Some elusive time in the future when we can slow down, when we're not just struggling to survive, when we're not just keeping our heads above water, then we can actually enjoy the ride. After I attain, acquire, get approval, find love, purchase, have kids, am successful, retire, die, become, after this current drama, after the next transition, or after everyone around me is doing well is when I will be able to feel okay. Then I can rest. Then I can relax and enjoy the experience. Then I can feel joy within each moment. Then I will feel good and can be truly happy, after, then, later, someday.

By succumbing to momentary defeat now, we are unconsciously acting out the patterns of our own victimization as our creation style. We think we have no personal choice to change our current state of being and our current perspective of our experience, so we renounce personal choice as victims to the current circumstances going on in our life. Our feelings are seemingly reactionary to whatever scenario the current circumstance may hold. If we're experiencing pleasant circumstances that match our expectations, we feel happy. If we're experiencing challenging, unpleasant circumstances, we feel stressed or unhappy. We are looking to change our circumstances thinking, which will change our core emotions. We're expressing that this very moment is not good enough and instead of shifting that perspective where it resides, at our core, we just surrender to the defeat of our soul's inner passion for now as an effort to gain the rewards later. We want to change the circumstances around us, because we think it will change our energetic state of being. We think we can change our disposition and the way we feel deep inside by changing the scenery. Being unaware that our current state of being is what manifests our physical experience, we are seemingly convinced it's the other way around. We are unconsciously manifesting struggle after struggle after struggle by ignoring or overlooking our core intentions, motives and our innermost desires and fears that exist right here and right now.

We may chase comforts and pleasures while avoiding all sources of discomfort and pain, because we are motivated by fear. We fear harm, whether bodily or emotional, etc. because we buy into a belief that tells us harm is inevitable or that we must act in a certain way in order to avoid individuals and circumstances that can take away our safety. We aren't completely living, expressing, and creating as the love of our inner heart space, but are living from a deeply imbedded fear that we aren't safe within our experience. Our core beliefs tell us our ultimate safety isn't guaranteed, so we must do something specific or work to protect ourselves from harm, and defend ourselves against outside forces that seek to hurt us. Protection, caution, defense, and seeking to avoid pain are all fear-based ideas created by buying into the false notion that our core essence is not inherently safe.

If we are striving for the idea of monetary security or freedom from the struggle, the energetic value we are embodying is one of not yet having or being, so our manifested reality will reflect the same level of lack and desperation we are engaging. If we are living to avoid pain or think we need fear, caution, and defense to protect ourselves from outside harm, we are personally creating a reality which reflects the notion that we are not safe, as that is the underlying fear we are engaging and emitting with our choices. If we give up our personal responsibility of choice to a system of authority or set ideology for a sense of external safety, it is because we fear our own choices and inner experience, so our physical life will reflect that same level of lack and insecurity.

True safety and security are only found within the core of our inner being, as alignment with our authentic essence, pure presence, and absolute awareness, where absolutely no lack exists at all. Our inner being and heart are directly connected to the eternal life force that creates worlds. The infinite flow of creation is our true core essence; we exist as unconditional love in expression. The entire universe is conspiring in our favor. There is absolutely nothing to fear.

The unconscious patterns of victimhood we participate in only occur because of unresolved fear we have in our energetic field because our core beliefs include the idea of lack as an absolute truth. The unresolved fears and fear of lack are, in essence, creating our experiences for us, because we have unconsciously renounced our personal free will by not choosing our current state of being within each Now moment. Our innermost fears are reflected as worry, doubt, and concern with our own personal experience, which translate into stress and struggle in our daily life. We may feel that who we are, our choices, and our life in general are not good enough, that we are not good enough just as we are, so we physically manifest that idea of lack, insecurity, struggle, and pain into our physical reality in which we live. When we live as a victim to our innermost fears, we are unconsciously creating the very demons we run from.

When we choose to face our inner self by peeling back the layers of fear and conditioning, we will reveal our authentically passionate and empowered self. When we courageously face our fears by walking through the pain and discomfort, without any resistance, and with complete acceptance of our most vulnerable aspects, we shed the light of awareness upon the deepest recesses of our psyche and transform the inner demons into angels. Fear has created shadows of illusion within our experience which we've been trying to avoid, deny, and resist. By turning the light of our awareness and attention inward and embracing all that is with the deepest compassion of our heart, we shed light onto that which was previously unseen, unknown, and feared. Now all the dark shadows of illusion are illuminated to show us where more presence, attention, and self-nurturing are necessary to heal our innermost pains. Love heals all fear and frees our innocence. Love mends all wounds. Self-love and nurturing resolve all insecurities.

All that we perceive as being distorted are the things we've kept hidden and dark expressing its pain. The most vulnerable, wounded aspects of our innocence desires our attention and unconditional love. We must allow all the emotions in our field to be fully felt. We must embrace all experiences as necessary for our learning, growth, and alignment, even the not so pleasant ones. Embracing all as aspects of love, and resisting none, is our key to freedom. Our denied wounded aspects yearn to be integrated into the love that is our authentic core being. By shining our awareness on and allowing all parts of our self-authentic expression, we will realize all that was feared was just the forsaken and unloved aspects of our very own being.

With our innermost fears resolved into love, we will know the true content of our heart and mind, which is the essence of love and, by default, when unconscious, the desire to be loved. We can consciously express from that awareness by manifesting from the overflowing love in our heart. By consciously choosing to align with the flow of infinite love within, our heart starts to sing of overflowing passion, joy, bliss, beauty, and freedom. Then our physical life starts reflecting those sweet energies of delight. When we start to choose love over fear each moment, and choose empowerment over being a victim, we are starting to create the life of our greatest dreams!

Our heart's innermost desires and our deepest soul yearnings need physical expression in order for our whole being to feel vibrantly alive and passionately invigorated. We feel lack and fear when we are out of alignment with our authentic core being. Our most authentic self seeks expression. This free-flowing, joy-filled, fundamental, core passion energy is total and complete love, and includes no fear at all. It is a physically embedded aspect of our most refined, sacred self, in order to move us towards more peace, more love, more authentic bliss and more creative expansion of our heart's greatest love song in this experience. This passion is where all our loving creative endeavors spring forth from, effortlessly. It's not striving because we feel lack, it's our creative heart song whispering it's tune all along and finally getting recognized by our awareness for full expression to be embarked upon. This is the tune our heart sings in the background the whole time, waiting to have its melody realized by us consciously, so we can sing, dance, create, and play along. This creative heart song is our manifestation being unveiled before our very eyes each and every day, aligning more and more with our truest expression of Self. It's our loving presence being more and more grounded into our physical body to express unconditional love to all of the world. It isn't striving at all; it's allowing, aligning, surrendering, playing, and effortlessly creating our hearts grandest dreams. There is no fear, limitations, lack, time constraints, doubt, or worry that goes along with our heart song, only the energetic purity of absolute freedom, joy, beauty, presence, being, and expressions of unconditional love.

We can choose to align ourselves with the infinite flow of creation, the force that manifests worlds. We can connect with the unshakable foundation of our inner power and then balance that with authentic outward expressions of our heart's deepest compassion. We can choose to extend beauty by shining our genuine radiance to all we interact with through the simplicity of a smile. We can artistically create a life of peace, joy, beauty, bliss, and magic with each conscious brush stroke, with each intentional breath we gratefully take, embracing all that exists right here and now. We may embody the most elegant and graceful poise of the finest dancer with each step we take and each action we make. We can create any experience we so choose simply by shifting the focus of our awareness. By consciously focusing on that which makes our heart sing, we will thrive abundantly and as ecstatically as our imagination will take us.

An ideal creation is one where we authentically share our heart with the world; share our passions, be, love, and create what makes our heart sing! A most worthy focus is to be aligned with absolute, unconditional love and expressing that overflowing love with self and all others we interact with each and every moment. Absolute love includes no fear, so resolving our deepest fears enables us more alignment with the purest energies of altruistic love. Being unconditionally loving means our huge, beautiful heart is completely wide open to all with no need for protection or expectation, and to embody and express gentle compassion, grace, dignity, reverence for and nurturance of self and all others we interact with. We can focus on allowing ourselves to be completely authentic at all times, because we are fearless and aligned with the essence of source creator, completely surrendering to the eternal essence of divinity that flows within as absolutely every aspect of our experience. By fully embracing each moment just as it is, while embodying the energies of pure love and gratitude, we are allowing the oneness, magic, freedom, and beauty that already exists within all to be realized by us, as a gorgeous display of infinite perfection unfolding before our very eyes. Our conscious focus upon unconditional love as our true essence in each moment and all our expressions (thoughts, words, actions, and choices) flowing from that solidified alignment will ultimately create paradise as our experience here on Earth.

***

To contact Anna:

Empowerment Coach, Intuitive Healer & Writer

http://www.ConsciousManifesting.com

anna@annaloveintuitive.com

https://www.facebook.com/annaloveintuitive

Colleen Williamson

Colleen, the youngest of four children, was raised by her mother. She learned the value of a dollar at a young age. This important life lesson taught her how to be resourceful and responsible, but it also instilled limiting beliefs. As a teenager, she found herself in an abusive relationship with the father of her two children. This experience impacted her life deeply; leaving her feeling trapped and unable to move forward for many years.

She lost her father to a painful battle with cancer, which ultimately led to her own diagnosis two years after his death. This experience became a turning point in her life. She discovered personal development and her journey of self-discovery began.

Colleen struggled for years trying to find success not only as an Online Marketer, but in various business ventures as well. An entrepreneur at heart, the limiting beliefs she carried around for years made it difficult to find the success she was looking for. She discovered the Robbins-Madanes Mastery Program, and became a Certified Coach.

Colleen's purpose is to inspire others to overcome their own limiting beliefs; allowing them to discover their dreams, goals, and true potential in their personal and professional lives.

You—The Unfinished Masterpiece

By Colleen Williamson

Life is a Gift

Challenges are a reality of life. How we choose to face them can make all the difference to what transpires in our future. Every day, we must strive to learn, grow, and become a better person; as well as to help create positive change in the lives of others. We only have this one life to live and it's up to us to create an incredible future and live a life without limits.

We all have a unique story; we have our past, our present and our yet to be created future. As I reflect back on all I have been through in my life, although experiencing some very trying times, there isn't much I would change. All the difficult challenges have made me who I am today. I have so much gratitude and deeply appreciate this incredible gift we are given called Life!

Our past can shape our destiny if we allow it to. We have the ability to choose our future and what path to take. The world is full of opportunity waiting to be realized by you, the artist of your journey!

Your Values Affect Your Life

In the vulnerable years of our childhood, we looked for guidance from the influential people in our lives. Our parents, teachers, and siblings all played a pivotal role in the framework of who we have become. We absorbed all that was going on around us, as we learned to shape our thoughts, and learned right from wrong. It is in these formative years that we created our belief systems and values, taking in information and storing it in our subconscious mind for future use.

We may begin to recognize that our learned values stemmed from both positive and negative thoughts and beliefs. These instilled beliefs that have been stored and played repeatedly in our minds, more often than not, have developed who we have become.

As well we may question some of the values we grew up with. We may decide to keep, change, or delete any of our past programming, if it no longer serves us. Discovering we have values of our own, and that we need to honor what is genuinely important to us, is crucial. If not, our lives can be unfulfilled. It is only when we come to the understanding that we have the ability to re-create who we are, if we so desire, can we then have life-changing breakthroughs.

Your Primary Question

Growing up, we may have been part of an awkward, embarrassing, or even traumatic situation. These life events have unknowingly created patterns in our lives that affect what and how we do things today. From this, a primary question is formed and becomes a part of who we are.

You may have memories of being teased in front of a group of friends, classmates, or family members. Perhaps you were rejected by your first love, or were a victim of bullying. In that very moment of stress, a statement, comment, or action directed toward you affected you very deeply. You took to heart those very painful words and absorbed them into your being. These traumatic experiences may have left you with feelings of shame, guilt, or unworthiness. Without knowing, these events often resulted in a question that you have asked yourself repeatedly in your mind, aloud or unconsciously. **This is your primary question**, which can also come in the form of a statement, that can paralyze you from moving forward and impair you from living a fulfilled life.

Your Primary Question or Statement could be:
- What is wrong with me?
- Why doesn't anything work for me?
- Why am I so stupid?
- Why am I such a procrastinator?
- I'm not good enough.

- I won't amount to anything.
- Nothing I do is ever good enough.
- No one will want to hear what I have to say.
- I don't even know and I don't even care.

Do any of these questions or phrases sound familiar to you? If not, are there others that come to mind? It is not uncommon that you will generate more than one question or statement; however, you may find that one will resonate more than the other.

The Effects of Your Primary Question

I was raised by my mother in a single-parent home. My parents divorced when I was only five years old. Coming from a family with very few luxuries, I learned at an early age the value of a strong work ethic and that one has to work hard for their money.

At the age of 18, I gave birth to a daughter; followed by a son, four years later. For nine years, I found myself in a mentally and physically abusive relationship with the father of my children. This experience left me feeling helpless, alone, and imprisoned; it caused me to remain stagnant for many years. Often having feelings of depression and desperation, I was exhausted from the continuous stress in my life. The words *"I Just Don't Know What To Do!"* spoken with such emotional intensity became so embedded in my subconscious. The impact of continually repeating these words grew stronger in my belief system. It became a key trigger, a negative motivating factor in my life.

This belief molded my future for years to come. As hard as I tried to attempt various business ventures, I couldn't find the success I truly wanted. I had big dreams to pursue, but I just couldn't find the confidence within myself to make them happen. The statement, **"I Just Don't Know What To Do!"** resulted in a fear of commitment, procrastination, and paralysis. These characteristics became a recurring pattern in my life. In hindsight, I now see the effects of my past so clearly!

Your Thoughts Become Your Reality

You may have heard the quote "What you think about you bring about." Through personal experience, I believe that all things happen for a reason due to our individual consistent thoughts. Events and circumstances are created by these ongoing thoughts. When negative thoughts plague our mind, negative events and situations come forth. These recurring events may leave us to believe that it is the only path we were meant to travel, that it is our destiny!

When I was 32 years old, my father passed away after a painful struggle with bone cancer. Multiple Myeloma took his life at the young age of 57. His death left me completely heartbroken. I was saddened to watch as he suffered in helplessness, trying to make the most of what he knew were his final months. I experienced feelings of great loss, anger, and abandonment; for him not only leaving me, but for leaving this world much too soon. The constant grieving over his death had created so much stress and intense emotion inside of me, that two years later, at the age of 34, I was diagnosed with Stage 3 Non-Hodgkin's Lymphoma. The tumor in my abdomen had grown to the size of a grapefruit. Frightened, and feeling detached from the world around me, the all-too-familiar statement "I Just Don't Know What To Do" resurfaced once again. My doctors started me on aggressive chemotherapy, but I was soon to learn the treatment plan wasn't working. Within a couple of months, my Stage 3 cancer had advanced to Stage 4. I continued with grueling treatments and a healing process that lasted 2 more years. From a cancer patient, I became a survivor, in more ways than one. I not only conquered the cancer, but this became a pivotal turning point in my life!

> *"When You* Change *The Way You Look at Things, The Things You Look at Change."*—Wayne Dyer

This inspiring and powerful quote by Wayne Dyer is one I reflect upon, often.

I know in my heart that I will continue to be cancer free. I strongly feel it was a stepping stone and a major part of my journey; one that I needed to experience in order to be where I am today. Since recovering, the incredible journey of self-discovery and personal development began. This led me on a path of self-awareness and I have never looked back! I've uprooted events from years past which uncovered deep emotional issues that needed closure. Most importantly, I have shone a light on why these events occurred and the effects they have had on my life.

The Journey of Self-Discovery

When we want to make an impact, we must first look within to create change, pushing through barriers that may block us from achieving our goals. Taught at a young age, that if you want the luxuries of life, you need to work hard and nothing comes for free. This created an entrepreneurial mindset within me. The desire to do something on a bigger scale was always forefront in my mind. I realized my purpose and passion is to help people live a life without limits. I also have a mission to act as a voice for homeless and abused animals, so they may have a better, more deserving life. Through the connection of like-minded people, who have a similar vision for global change, together we can make an impact in a bigger way.

Knowing firsthand the challenges and obstacles of building a business and working towards personal goals, one must believe in themselves in order to achieve success. Overcoming the lack of confidence, and the fear of talking to people, was a difficult challenge for me. This fear made me want to give up hundreds of times. There finally came a time where the scales tipped the other way—my good days began to outnumber the bad ones. Everything somehow became easier and began to fall into place. The bigger vision became so clear; and with persistence, determination, and always having the end goal in mind, I found the belief in myself to make it all happen

Throughout my own personal development journey, I incorporate two powerful forms of Emotional Freedom Technique (EFT), Tapping, and Neuroplasticity. Tapping is a combination of Ancient Chinese Acupressure and Modern Psychology that work together to physically alter your brain, energy system, and body, all at once. The practice consists of tapping with your fingertips on specific meridian points while talking through traumatic memories and a range of emotions. Neuroplasticity is defined as the brain's ability to reorganize itself by forming new neural connections throughout life. Neuroplasticity is the process in which your brain's neural pathways are altered as an effect of environment, behavioral, and neuro changes. By incorporating a technique called future rehearsal, we learn to change our thoughts, by rehearsing in our mind what we want in our life. Both EFT strategies have helped millions of people around the world.

Tapping and Neuroplasticity are a part of my personal daily routine. I include these modalities into my coaching programs. As a certified graduate of the "Robbins-Madanes Mastery Coaching Program—Strategic Intervention," I have learned invaluable skills about non-conventional strategies in personal development and life change from top industry leaders Tony Robbins and world-renowned Psychologist Cloe Madanes. We cannot work toward rebuilding our future until we peel back the layers and uncover what is buried deep within our subconscious mind. This journey of self-discovery is an incredible mountain to conquer and is one I continue to climb daily. Because of this journey, "I **DO** Know What to Do!" I now have an awareness of my primary question and it no longer rules my life!

My Promise to You

In the areas of personal development, life change, and business growth, I am dedicated to motivate, inspire, and push you beyond what you never thought possible. I will also share with you how to use proven Online Systems, that will work for any business. If you are an entrepreneur, coach, speaker, or Network Marketer, I will work with you to overcome the obstacles which may prevent you from achieving your goals.

I dedicate this chapter to people who may come from similar circumstances and strive for change. For those people who want more out of life and have a similar vision, but continue to face roadblocks that limit them from moving forward, I am here to help break down those barriers and discover the triggers that limit you from having the success that you desire and rightfully deserve. When you have breakthroughs in your personal life, you can then have success in all areas of your life!

Here's to Your Success,

***

To Contact Colleen:

www.colleenwilliamsoncoaching.com

www.onlinewithcolleen.com

email: colleen@onlinewithcolleen.com

email: collwilliamson@gmail.com

<u>Find me on Social Media</u>

Facebook: facebook.com/colleen.williamson.758

Facebook Business Page: facebook.com/ColleenWilliamsonCoaching/

Twitter: collwilliamson

Instagram: onlinewithcolleen

LinkedIn: linkedin.com/in/colleen-williamson

Pinterest: pinterest.com/workwithcolleen/

YouTube: youtube.com/c/ColleenWilliamsonOnline

Skype: colleenawilliamson

Janna Hoiberg

A renowned international speaker, workshop facilitator, and author, Janna Hoiberg has personally led thousands of business owners to success and inspired thousands more during her 35-year career. Janna specializes in *creating a path for the next generation family business.* Her passion is working with families actively navigating the transition path while still running the business, helping one generation step away and the next generation to take the lead. A gifted teacher and stirring presenter, Janna ignites audiences and teams with her proven strategies to elevate communication, leadership, and team building.

Janna is recognized throughout the U.S. as an author and thought leader in the unique circumstances of businesses owned and managed by one or more family members. Her book *The Family Business*: *How to be in Business with People You Love, Without Hating Them* is a critically acclaimed, insightful compendium of her learning throughout decades of running businesses, speaking, and working with business owners who just happen to be related to each other. Her latest book *The Backpackers Guide to Business Success: Thriving in the Wilderness of Business* parallels the joys and challenges of mountaineering with those of business.

The Effect of Attitude on Altitude

By Janna Hoiberg

We live in Colorado and hike at high elevations where we have less oxygen compared with our previous sea-level home. Physical activity that might be fairly easy at lower elevations becomes, you might say, more "breath-taking" up here.

When I first moved to Colorado, I went for a walk at 8,500 feet. I kept thinking to myself, "I am in worse shape than I thought. I am so short of breath it's ridiculous." Then the light dawned: the problem wasn't me. (Well it was, just not in the way I initially thought.) It was the elevation. I needed time to adjust to high-altitude breathing.

At high altitudes, physical activity—like running up a mountain—is more difficult. If you cannot allow time to acclimate completely, your pace must be adjusted. Another option is to work out so hard and get in such good shape at your low altitude hometown that your body can manage the change in elevation. For people who are particularly sensitive, all of these techniques taken together might be a good idea. Some people are not bothered at all; others can have significant effects due to altitude sickness.

The effect of altitude on athletic performance is one of the reasons that the United States Olympic Center (USOC) is located in Colorado Springs. Because there is relatively little oxygen at high altitudes, people who live there produce more red blood cells than people at lower altitudes. When athletes train at high altitudes and then travel to lower altitudes for competitions, they are better conditioned (and better prepared) than people from lower elevations. They have more endurance because their bodies receive more oxygen via more red blood cells.

Our attitude affects our professional lives in the same way elevation (or altitude) affects physical activity. Even a simple activity at work can be quite difficult or stressful if approached with a negative attitude, and difficult situations (which come with stress built in) require outstanding positive attitudes to be handled effectively. We need to prepare for work challenges and adapt our attitudes in much the same way that our bodies adjust to the challenge of high altitudes.

Backpackers prepare for physical challenges in much the same way professionals prepare for business and career challenges—in advance of the situation and consistently. When preparing for a backpacking trip, we know that anyone coming with us must be physically prepared to handle the rigors of the trail. Someone's first backpacking trip should not be a five-day journey with a 4,000-foot elevation gain. We start with a short weekend trip—to shake out what they know and what they can handle.

This type of shake-out trip was always fun with Boy Scouts. There was almost always one scout who would bring a cooler of food and a lot of cans (which are heavy), enough food to feed the entire troop for a week! This scout would trudge along, weighed down, and start complaining about 200 feet onto the trail.

As leaders, we would caution scouts, parents, and anyone who would listen not to over-pack, but it never failed; at least one scout brought along everything including the kitchen sink. Such mishaps are what stories are made of and how people learn, but such a situation would be disastrous on a five-day trip. We take a short trip the first time so the lesson can be learned.

Preparation is not just about packing, of course; it also involves physical conditioning. Experienced backpackers know that going all winter without doing any physical workout, exercise, or activity and then just heading out on a trail results in sore legs, groaning, and general unpleasantness. So we work out all winter. That Stairmaster is not my friend, but to my body it resembles the steps on a mountain. Those core-building classes at the gym are good for my health, although I usually question their value about forty minutes into the class.

As we look at personal and business goals, here is a perspective from Darren Hardy, author of *The Entrepreneur Roller Coaster*: "This is my mountain and I'm going all the way to the top! You are either going to see me waving from the summit or lying dead on the side. I am not coming back!"

The above quote should not be taken too literally. Darren Hardy is not trying to make light of actual mountain-climbing accidents, and neither am I. The number of deaths each year from hiking is not compiled in one place, yet anecdotal evidence says it is fairly high. And the possibility of such outcomes is something I take quite seriously. I know that to hike a mountain, climb a fourteener, or ski down a mountain you need to have training. You need to be both mentally and physically prepared. Without preparation, the end of your journey may not be what you envisioned.

You must prepare for business and career as well. It is your job to continue your training in your field so you can attack your mountain. I can climb mountains, but I should not ever try to swim the English Channel, frame a house, or run a steel mill. They aren't my skillsets or passions. Unless I got a lot of training first, I would fail.

Serious mountaineers who risk their lives climbing mountains do so simply because they love the challenge. The point of the quote is that anybody who sets a substantial goal will face difficulty, and determination will be necessary. Think about Tommy Caldwell and Kevin Jorgeson climbing Yosemite's Dawn Wall and making history. (Nineteen days after setting out to achieve one of climbing's most difficult challenges, Tommy and Kevin reached the summit of the 3,000-foot rock known as El Capitan in Yosemite National Park.)

Whether he was aware of the Darren Hardy quote or not, Tommy Caldwell took the idea to heart. He was determined to let nothing stop him. It took him many tries to achieve his goal, yet he made it to the top, something that no one else in history had ever done! Yet his climbing career has had a cost, over and above time and money. While climbing in Uzbekistan, he was captured by rebels; he lost a finger, which probably should have ended his career as a climber; and he ended up in divorce. Yet the setbacks never stopped him.

What stops you? How badly do you want to achieve your goal, and what are you willing to give up achieving it?

Fear is what stops many people. There are many shades of fear. Two acronyms that express opposite viewpoints on fear are:

Forget Everything And Run

Face Everything And Rise

Does either of these acronyms reflect your way of dealing with fear?

The concept of choosing a goal and sticking with it is important. Then, after setting a goal, you must plan, prepare, and lay the appropriate foundation to achieve success. You also must understand the potential risks associated with your plan.

If a mountaineer is going to invest in climbing a mountain but doesn't want to end up being the one who gets rescued because of lack of preparation, he or she must plan, develop the necessary skills, and perform critical thinking tasks in order to address the risks. The same is true in business and career. If you are going to invest all your savings on a single business venture, you'd better understand the risks. Otherwise, you might face the harsh reality of totally starting over.

The owner of a potential startup company asked me for input on a product he thought would be fantastic. He had made prototypes and received great feedback and encouragement to get the product manufactured. He was ready and now needed to understand how to launch this product. I advised him that he still needed to do planning and homework. Was there another product on the market like his? What would it take to manufacture his product? What price would his customer be willing to pay for this product? Those three questions prompted a call back to me saying that he was shelving his idea. There was already a product much like his on the market, and the cost to manufacture his design was greater than the prospective customers were willing to pay. As a result of investigating the risks, he chose to go a different route. Answering those simple questions kept him from making a costly business mistake.

People who don't understand the risks they face are likely to make foolish mistakes. We climbed a fourteener once with a teenager who didn't believe he needed to bring a warm coat and gloves; after all, the temperature was warm at the base. Trust me—it wasn't warm at the top! He needed a coat and gloves. Fortunately, we were prepared and had additional layers that we could share. Admittedly, we didn't anticipate the gale-force winds at the top, either. You cannot always predict the weather at the top of a mountain any more than you can always predict future business conditions. On that mountain, the teenager learned a very valuable lesson; now he never hikes without adequate preparation and gear. Isn't that like most life lessons? Often we don't truly learn until we are faced with the results of poor decisions. Then we tend to do better next time.

Preparation and risk-assessment doesn't mean you can't be flexible. Life happens, and business must be flexible. But sometimes the need for flexibility is used as an excuse. Stop using excuses! Determine your goals and stick with them. Many people turn around and give up on a mountain about eighty percent of the way to the top. They miss the sense of success, the beauty, and the accomplishment they would attain if they were to stick with their goal. The same thing often happens in business. You must make the decision.

Are you truly committed?

What could stand in your way?

Are you prepared for the consequences of possible failure?

What will you do if or when you fail?

What will keep you moving forward?

On a mountain, altitude can affect our ability to perform to our usual standards. We had two teenage friends from New England (sea level) stay with us for a week. We made sure they had a few days to get acclimated and then headed up to the mountains to camp one night and hike the next. One of the kids, Joel, wasn't drinking sufficient water and probably not getting enough electrolytes. He started getting altitude sickness on the way up, and we had to turn back. Fortunately, his attitude was good, even when the altitude was creating issues. We chose to turn back, making the joke that if we wanted to know how to get back to camp we could just follow the places where he threw up. The truth is, even without altitude sickness, we weren't prepared to hike across a wide open space covered with twelve to eighteen inches of snow. For me, the decision to turn back was rooted in a desire to not need a rescue with two teenagers on a high mountain. We all had a good time, even though we were not able to reach our goal. That day, staying flexible and safe were the most important elements of our success (arriving at the base whole and together). Attitude was the most important element in doing it all pretty happily.

Getting rescued on a mountain is not a bad thing; it is far better than loss of life or limb. Yet, the more you push through challenges, the better the journey. On the other hand, the more excuses you make, the less enjoyable and successful the journey is likely to be. The better prepared I am for the climb, the better I do on the trail. I can hike faster, breathe better, feel better, and therefore climb farther and faster. What preparation are you doing on a regular basis for the "hills" at work? A little preparation each day—even if it is fifteen minutes of reading books that challenge your mind and thought process to get you out of your box and your comfort-zone thinking—may be the difference between getting and not getting that next job or promotion. The choice is yours.

We had a local election with a very poor turnout among young people. One of the candidates was young, qualified, and should have won. Why didn't he win? Partly because not enough voters in his age group actually got out to vote. The local newspaper asked the millennials why they didn't vote. They had *excuses*: "The ballots needed to be mailed, and I didn't have stamps." "Why can't we vote online like we do everything else?" Most anyone reading this will agree they are excuses. There are tons of places to buy stamps, just get out and do it.

The Change[11]

I can hear the laughter now from anyone over forty for that second excuse. "Get out the door, kids! There is a whole three-dimensional world out there!"

Although I loathe excuses, I also have learned to strip them down to see what I can learn. Where is the grain of truth? How can I use that grain of truth, turning it into something useful to improve the business? How can I eliminate the excuse? Maybe the lesson from those millennials (the grain of truth for the rest of us) is that traditions are changing more quickly than in any previous generation. If you want to keep up, you must understand the changes and how those changes will impact your business and career.

Athletes train before they head to competition. They seldom coast. Businesspeople and entrepreneurs need to train, too. How often do you train? Every day? What have you done to prepare for the journey ahead? Let's look at a couple of questions to help you evaluate your training process:

Do you plan for your day? Or do you just show up and react?

Before a big job interview or sales appointment, do you practice your interview skills? Or do you wing it?

Do you walk through every sales presentation (out loud) before you present? Statistics show that less than half of salespeople practice their presentations. Yet a salesperson's closing rate is directly proportional to their preparation.

Do you document your negotiating points before a vendor meeting? Or do you wait to see what they want first?

Do you stage that big customer meeting? Do you go out of your way to understand the customer's perspective?

The following story shows what a little preparation can mean. I had the opportunity many years ago to negotiate with the Boston Red Sox. They were purchasing software from us, and it was a big deal. We were negotiating in the conference room that overlooked Fenway

Park. The Red Sox's reps sat us down at the table so we could see Fenway, the Boston skyline, and the surrounding area. They sat so they looked at the wall behind us.

Two lessons were learned that day. One was on focus. Who do you think was more likely to get distracted? We were! Not only that: We wanted the deal more and more as we looked out at the view of Fenway Park. The distraction could have been a real issue if we hadn't prepared for the negotiation. We knew our bottom line. We knew what was important and what wasn't important. We could have gotten distracted, but our preparation ensured we remained on target. The second lesson that day included seating positions around a table. Where we sat did make a difference. We were very well prepared, and as a result, we ended up with a deal that worked for both organizations.

Preparation had another effect when one of our sea-level friends came to visit for a week. We conscientiously spent a couple of days in Colorado Springs before heading to Vail, a town located much higher in the mountains. Nevertheless, by the time we got there, we had to head directly to the emergency room as she was unable to breath and panicky because of it. Her husband and daughter were quite fine, showing no effects from the altitude. She had recognized that she didn't feel the best shortly after she arrived, yet she didn't recognize that it was altitude sickness. Without our time in Colorado Springs, her ability to adapt to a higher elevation would have been even harder.

With altitude sickness, you have no control; some bodies simply react that way when faced with reduced oxygen. Even a person who gets altitude sickness one time might return to the high altitude and have no effects from it. (Though it may take some convincing to get my friend to return!) Altitude sickness is both uncontrollable and unpredictable.

As much as my friend was affected by the altitude, her attitude was always good. She continued to participate in as many activities as possible. She just brought along her companion—an oxygen tank—to every activity. She didn't hike many trails with us, but anything she could do, she did. She could easily have sat in the condo complaining all day. She could have insisted that everybody stay back with her, ruining the trip for both families. But her positive attitude meant that everybody finished the experience with many positive memories.

Just as we cannot always control our body's reactions, we don't always have control of the world outside ourselves. The economic climate can change; we cannot control that. We can be struck down by the flu the day of a big presentation; we cannot control that either. But we can always control our attitude in the face of both personal and professional challenges.

Excerpt from: *The Backpackers Guide to Business Success: Thriving in the Wilderness of Business*

***

To contact Janna:

Email: Janna@JannaHoiberg.com

Phone: 719-358-6936

Website: www.JannaHoiberg.com

Twitter: www.twitter.com/jannahoiberg

LinkedIn: https://www.linkedin.com/in/jannahoiberg?trk=nav_responsive_tab_profile

Facebook: http://facebook.com/familybusinessspecialist

Todd Mauney

With a natural talent and passion for empowering business leaders, Todd Mauney has built a successful career as a professional coach, entrepreneur, trainer, speaker, and author. He is founder and president of ROI Coaching Solutions, a coaching consultancy offering proven methodologies for financial advisors and industry business owners to grow by more than 30% annually.

Todd believes everyone is endowed with unique, God-given strengths. For over 15 years, he has helped thousands of clients identify and harness these gifts to achieve greater prosperity and more fulfilling lives.

Prior to starting ROI Coaching Solutions, Todd founded two successful marketing businesses and co-founded ProAdvisor Coach, Light of Christ Methodist Church and Shepherd Care, a cutting-edge international leadership coaching program for clergy. Early in his career, Todd received numerous national sales and leadership accolades from Fortune 500 powerhouses Pitney Bowes, Konica, and ADP.

Todd resides in Charlotte, NC with his wife and three children. He has a business degree from East Carolina University, professional coach certification from International Coach Academy, and is a Certified Fire-walking Instructor.

Todd enjoys time with family, sports, the outdoors, and staying active within his church and community.

A Dichotomy for Prosperity
"Breathing In" and "Breathing Out."

By Todd Mauney

"From the beginning of time, God established a rhythm of life—of being and doing—of breathing in and breathing out which is essential for the sustaining of all life. However, we have often adopted our own alternative rhythm of doing, doing, doing—of breathing out, breathing out, breathing out."

— **Beth M. Crissman,** *Plowpoint*

An Introduction

The dichotomy of "breathing in" and "breathing out" applies to all aspects of our lives. It is a powerful natural and universal law of rhythm seen in a variety of contexts and circumstances with profound implications for our physical, emotional, spiritual, relational, and professional prosperity. By recognizing how this law is playing out for you, understanding how it works, and investing a few minutes to complete the simple exercises I provide in this chapter, you can achieve better results with less stress and greater ease.

To begin understanding the power behind this principle, it will be helpful to consider some other well-known contrasting perspectives. We are all familiar with:

- Doing vs. Being
- Pushing vs. Pulling (or attracting)
- Sewing vs. Reaping
- Hunting vs. Farming
- Working "on" vs. working "in"

Each perspective takes on a different connotation based on the context in which it is applied; yet they all have something in common...*oscillation*. According to *Wikipedia*, "Oscillations occur not only in mechanical systems, but also in dynamic systems in virtually every area of science: for example, the beating human heart, business cycles in economics, predator-prey population cycles in ecology, geothermal geysers in geology, vibrating strings in musical instruments, periodic firing of nerve cells in the brain, and the periodic swelling of Cepheid variable stars in astronomy." Managing these oscillations is a central theme in life and essentially the heartbeat that sustains and enhances it.

So many of us today become trapped in a seemingly endless state of "imbalance" where, like a sound wave, there is more noise than music. Can you relate? Take for instance, a business owner caught up in the daily grind of working "IN" rather than "ON" their enterprise. It is from this "breathing out" perspective that most of us experience the greatest imbalance, so that is where we will focus first.

The concept of Breathing Out

When the human body is deprived of oxygen, it will suffer terrible mental and physical consequences known as hypoxemia or hypoxia. As Beth points out in the opening quote, when we are doing, doing, doing all the time, it is like breathing out without taking in life-giving oxygen. Fortunately, our brain is hardwired to breathe in, but can you imagine only breathing out? Yet, that is how many people live their lives, run their businesses, and even lead; all metaphorically breathing out...doing, doing, and doing all the time without taking a breath.

Relating the "doing" modality into life and work, society praises massive action because as renowned life coach Tony Robbins puts it, "Action is the most important key to any success." And do we not all want success?

Many measure success by their posessions. But is there more to it? Do not get me wrong; we all love cool things. However, we often stay so busy doing, we miss out on what we long for the most like happiness, purpose, fulfillment, connection, and joy. Unfortunately, with society becoming increasingly addicted to perpetual motion and constant doing, more people are suffering from a myriad of physical, psychological, emotional, and relational dysfunctions.

Even as we see these consequences in our own lives and those around us, far too many stay on the treadmill of perpetual doing, running as fast as they can towards a mirage of success. Relating this to business and life, there is a central point. *We must be aware and more intentional to strike a dynamic balance in order to be truly successful and prosperous.*

Like hypoxia, all this breathing out…doing, doing, doing…is "killing" us. We become confused by the dizzying pace at which we do things. One of the greatest thought leaders of our time, Peter Drucker, put it this way: "There is nothing as useless as doing efficiently that which should not be done at all." The doing itself becomes the focus rather than the purpose for which it is being done. In life and business, without the intention to balance this cycle, neither success nor significance can be fully realized.

Working mostly with the business sector and its leaders, I see the dysfunction of perpetual doing all the time. It breaks my heart to see determined business owners grinding away day to day, sacrificing so much to climb a mountain they later realize may have been the wrong one. They have the work ethic, but fail to plan and unknowingly plan to fail. They are busy doing, but not necessarily the right things because there is no time to slow down, "take a breath," and nurture themselves and their businesses.

> *"One of my favorite cartoons; a sad, depressing story about a pathetic Coyote who spends every waking moment of his life in the futile pursuit of a sadistic roadrunner, who mocks him and laughs at him as he's repeatedly crushed and maimed!"*
>
> — **George Newman**, *UHF*

It was fun to watch Wile E. Coyote chase Road Runner every Saturday morning as a child, but it must have really stunk to be him! And that is exactly how many of us feel chasing the wrong things, always busy trying to do something else to achieve something more. This is what breathing out, the constant "doing" paradigm, amounts to for so many. If this is hitting home for you, take heart. *There is hope in restoring a healthy rhythm and in doing so, achieving much greater prosperity in life and business.*

Self-Application

Figuratively speaking, where are you seeing signs of hypoxia like fatigue, forgetfulness, mental fog, irritability, burnout and other symptoms of constant doing or breathing out? The "Balance Wheel of Life" is one popular and powerful tool used by coaches to help assess one's sense of satisfaction and balance within eight areas of their life.

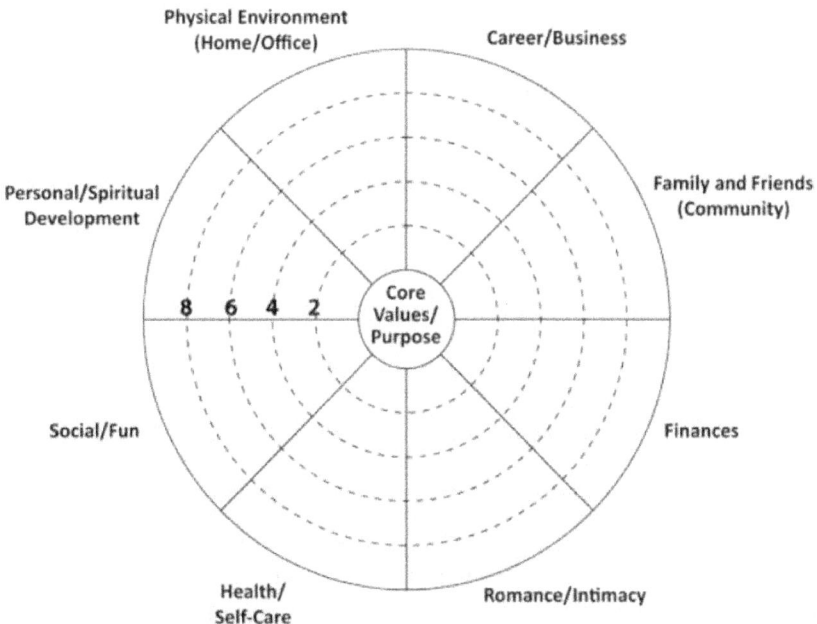

Simply think about the amount of exertion you're applying to these different areas. Shade each slice or area of your life from the center point out to the level you feel represents the amount of effort you're applying to it.

So if you feel you're pushing, working extremely hard, and exerting tremendous energy towards your financial circumstances, you'd shade "Finances" all the way out to the outer circle. If you feel you're applying minimal energy and exertion on this area, you may only shade to the first circle outside of the center.

Once completed, you will see how much energy you're exerting in each of these areas, which then begs the question, how is it improving the quality of your life at a core level?

If you are exerting a tremendous amount of energy without seeing how it is truly bringing more peace, joy, and happiness to your life, perhaps the time has come to consider the other side of this dichotomy.

Let's now look at what it means to "breathe in" and how to get better results from your "doing" efforts.

The concept of Breathing In

Popeye, the Sailor Man, is a fictional cartoon character who first appeared in comic strips and later animated cartoons during the 1930s. Each episode featured Popeye facing seemingly insurmountable challenges and taking a beating by his arch nemesis, Bluto. Down for the count, beaten up by Bluto and overwhelmed by the odds of victory, Popeye would reach for his trusty can of spinach and suddenly become super normal. His energy would explode, fear became courage, and solutions to his problems became immediately clear. He would then perform amazing feats of daring to overcome his obstacles, defeat his enemy, and win the girl, Olive Oyl.

Though Popeye is not a real person, we can learn a lot from his character. There are many times when we have more than we can handle and the "Blutos" of life beat us down. Like Popeye, we work hard trying to do all the right things, only to feel defeated or out of steam. Yet, we also have sources of energy, inspiration, and innovation we can access. "Breathing in" is metaphorically about eating our spinach; taking in the oxygen of life and accessing the best of who we are as human "beings" in order to "do" and "be" better. Popeye's spinach didn't change who he was at the core of his being, but rather expanded it! As a result, he was fully ALIVE and could do amazing things!

The concept of "breathing in" vs. "breathing out" is analogous with being vs. doing. We talked about doing, but what does it mean to "be" in order to "do" better? Think about it—we do not call ourselves human "doings" but rather human "beings." There is a reason for this. It is commonplace for us to think of the human body as merely an elaborate machine, but we are much more. Understanding who we are as "beings" is the gateway for our "doing" and achieving much more!

Fully grasping this will accelerate achievement and prosperity in all you do. It creates a state of "flow" seen in great athletes like Adrian Peterson, LeBron James, Shaun White, or Lionel Messi. And it is in the "breathing in" or "being" state that contributes most to flow, what is also referred to as being in the "zone."

Our "Being"

In his book, *The Pearl Beyond Price*, A.H. Almaas suggests, "At a certain age, very early on in life, each one of us becomes aware of himself or herself as a walking, talking, thinking, and feeling being—in short, as a living person. It is such a luminous discovery, but it quickly becomes dull with familiarity. Then we live our lives as if we now know what it is to be human, as if maturing were only a matter of becoming more of what we think we are already. The mystery is gone, and life becomes tedious and repetitive."

Consequently, we shift from self-discovery to looking for answers, solutions, peace, happiness, purpose, and joy from external sources…people, places, and things. Herein lies the temptation for perpetual "doing" in hopes of attaining more, but often falling short and feeling depleted.

There is something magical about connecting with our "being," who we really are, and our current reality. Through the power of self-awareness, we become more grateful for what we have, clear about what we really want and focused on how to make it happen with greater ease and joy. This applies to our personal and professional lives.

While facilitating a long, arduous strategy meeting with an executive team one day, we became exhausted from pushing ("breathing-out"), stuck with poor options and indecision. Mindful of what was happening, I suggested we take a literal and figurative "breath of fresh air" by continuing our brainstorming session while walking around our building.

Within minutes, a natural flow was restored. Everyone became clearer, innovative ideas started rolling out, and decisions were made. This example of "breathing in" illustrates how quickly energy and flow can be restored leading to amazing breakthroughs. This "breathing in" modality leads to better and more efficient decisions, which allows us to apply renewed energy ("doing") more effectively, resulting in improved outcomes.

A great man dying from a rare form of bone cancer provides yet another example of "breathing in" from a life perspective. "Being still allows us to focus and reflect on our blessings and allows the Lord to speak to us."

He goes on to say how important it is for him to "find a quiet 10 minutes to be open to the Lord, to speak to or to be still and know." Then he sums it up nicely by saying, "this is often so difficult in our busy, hectic world, but so necessary. My still time is each night in bed, spending time in prayer and reflection. This is my peace and *re-priming* of my 'Spiritual Pump' in ending the day and preparing for the next."

Self-Application

We see how energy is processed in a continuum…energy in, energy out. In the same way, we have become more aware of where we have exerted energy and now gained a better understanding of our need to replenish it.

With an open mind for discovery, I invite you to answer a few questions regarding your own life and work. Write your answers down somewhere to reflect on later:

- What does "breathing in" mean to you where you feel most energized, resourceful, and in a state of flow?
- How has "breathing in" improved your decision making, actions, and results?
- How can you be more intentional to "breathe in" more frequently and effectively?
- How would being more intentional to "breathe in" improve your personal and professional life?
- What will you commit to do starting NOW to strike a better balance and flow?

Reflecting on the earlier "balance wheel" exercise, consider that each area of your life may require a slightly different way of "being" or "breathing in" to restore energy, clarity, flow, and inspiration. Take relationship for instance. "Breathing in" might mean simply letting go of your agenda, seeking to fully listen and understand others better before trying to be understood, as the late Stephen Covey would say. As a result, both parties experience greater trust and connection which leads to a more productive relationship and better results from what you "do" together.

Another instance is finance, specifically earning more money. Perhaps you're pushing as hard as you can to generate more sales and convince people to buy your products. By pausing to "breathe-in," you might step back to more clearly define your ideal audience, get their input, develop your skills, and/or create a better strategy to make your sales efforts ("doing") more effective.

Consider a business owner or leader ready to launch a major growth initiative. Understanding this principle might motivate her or him to invest more time "being" with the employees to understand where they are emotionally and what they need in order to "do" the right things for rapid growth.

There are many applications for this process. The key is to understand that BOTH—"Breathing in" and "Breathing out," "Being" and "Doing"—are necessary to be maximally effective in life and business.

The Process Changes Everything

Use the "Balance Wheel of Life" to help you identify areas where excessive "doing" may be blocking you from a greater life and business experience. As you pay closer attention to how this dichotomy is showing up for you, let your emotions provide insight. Like instrumentation on an airplane, they will tell you if you are flying too high, low, fast, or slow so you can make adjustments.

Answer the questions in the second self-application section of this chapter to discover your own ways of "breathing in" and apply them to the life areas of the "Balance Wheel" where you want to make progress. Physically, you might eat healthier, sleep longer, or exercise more. In relationships, it might mean being a better listener, asking more than telling. At work, you could gather new information, set better goals, and develop smarter plans. Look for ways to improve what you "DO."

While most people experience dysrhythmia with excessive "breathing out" and "doing," it is important to recognize when the opposite extremes can be equally problematic. We can also spend too much time "breathing in"; indecisive and unproductive with a lack of results.

If you notice yourself saying, "it will all work out in time" or "I'm just trusting it will be ok," yellow flags should go up. It is good to trust God, the universe, or your source of faith; however, if you see a pattern of indecision and inaction, this attitude may be masking fear of failure or some other resistance. If you suspect this might be happening, repurpose your "breathing in" time to focus on what the resistance might be, seek input from a coach, and develop a strategy to move forward with accountability.

The choice to walk down this path of self-discovery and intention is an individual one. It can be difficult and frustrating to recognize and interrupt unhealthy habits of excessive "breathing out" (doing) or "breathing in" (being). Consequently, it is important to be patient with yourself as you discover where dysrhythmia is causing unwanted results and set new goals to find dynamic balance. Find your source of self-compassion, understanding, and grace as you make changes. Seek out a professional coach to reveal blind spots and empower you with new strategies. And like any goal, constantly remind yourself of the payoff for perseverance.

Be encouraged, knowing there is a domino effect where improvements in one area of your life will lead to improvements in other areas. As a colleague coach put it, "how you do anything is how you do everything." The key is to start somewhere, build momentum, and form new habits.

With motivation to leverage this powerful principle of prosperity, I encourage you to take the next step. Without judging or shaming, invest a few minutes today to assess your rhythm and identify one specific way to strike a better balance, improve your results, and experience greater prosperity.

Please visit my website, where you will find additional resources to help you further assess where you are, clarify where you want to be, and develop a game plan to get there. You can also learn more about what a professional coach can do to help you accelerate results. These resources are FREE at www.myroicoach.com. You can also access them and connect with me through LinkedIn. Just search my name and request to connect. If I can support you further, especially in growing your business with greater ease, please contact me through my website, LinkedIn profile, or email. We all have one life to live, and I want you to live your best one NOW!

***

To Learn More About or Contact Todd:

Website: www.myroicoach.com

Website: www.roicoachingsolutions.com

Website: www.7pillarsofprosperity.com

LinkedIn: https://www.linkedin.com/in/toddmauney

Business: 704-634-3180

Carolyn J. Rivera

Carolyn Rivera is a motivational speaker, leadership trainer, learning and development executive, reality television star, and author. Carolyn's professional career is rooted in the corporate world where she has worked for Fortune 50 companies for over 25 years. Her personal areas of expertise include leadership development, learning and development, talent management, performance management, operations, and linking performance to business results. Leadership is a passion for Carolyn and she has used her talent to help organizations achieve results far beyond their initial expectations. Her personal success is attributed to her need to constantly learn and grow. Carolyn is committed to mastering her own personal leadership first. By leading herself to achieve more, pushing her own limits, and eliminating obstacles she has become an effective leader capable of transferring her talent to management teams and organizations to achieve great results.

Carolyn auditioned for *Survivor* for four years before she was selected as a candidate. She was tireless in her ambition and motivation, which was ultimately recognized when she finished as runner up. Carolyn thrived as a contestant on *Survivor*. Carolyn's background in leadership aided her in her success, as she was accustomed to pushing beyond her personal limits.

Are You Nearsighted or Farsighted in Your Personal Vision?

By Carolyn J. Rivera

Whether you are a motivated leader of one or a fearless leader of many, you owe it to yourself to have a vision. After all, I'd like to think we're all put on this earth to kick life's butt just a little bit (or perhaps a lot, your choice). Regardless of whether you aspire to be a "big kicker" (you know who you are) or a "little kicker," most of us find ourselves at the same crossroad trying to grasp that elusive vision. Some of us jump in the car and get to the crossroad immediately, just to sit there for days or years without deciding to turn left or right; others of us take years to start the journey but enjoy the feel of our foot on the gas and the wind in our hair once we get the courage to leave the garage. So, it's no surprise that the most critical (and sometimes difficult) aspect to defining yourself as a leader is creating the vision.

If you consult *Webster* or one of its online counterparts (who clearly had a greater vision of how people would access dictionaries in the digital age), you will find a variety of definitions of vision. Some say it is something imagined, a vivid picture in your mind; others define it as a thought or concept formed by the imagination. Now, let's pop out of *Webster*'s world for a moment and ask ourselves if the definition of vision truly matters. Personally, I'd say no. While it is important to understand the concept, the actual definition only matters to the extent that it is adaptable to your reality and allows you to define your personalized vision. In practice, visions are out of reach at present and not easily attainable, but yet achievable and personally motivating.

Years ago, I read a *Harvard Business Review* article titled "Building Your Company's Vision" by Jim Collins and Jerry I. Porras. It stuck with me because it clearly broke down the steps to creating a vision. This particular article was geared toward the workplace, but its two main points are applicable to everyone. Collins and Porras stated that the first step toward a vision is to define what you stand for and why you exist, and the second step to creating a vision is to articulate your aspirations for the future. In a business setting, a vision could link to revenue goals, market penetration, and increased customer satisfaction. In a personal setting, the possibilities are endless. Regardless of the setting, the single most important element is to define your vision. By doing so and articulating it clearly, you will create the synergy necessary to achieve your vision. This holds true whether you are that motivated leader of one or the fearless leader of many I mentioned earlier.

Reflecting on this article several years later, I've developed a specific, five-step process to guide you through Collins and Porras' first two steps—and take it a few steps further to assist you through the implementation of your vision. *These are the steps on how to bring a vision to life:*

- Develop the vision
- Define the vision and expected outcomes
- Visualize success of your end game
- Communicate the vision with passion and energy
- Build a movement of inspired implementers

Step 1: Develop the Vision

For many people, developing a vision is a very difficult task. To be honest, I think many people get lost in the visioning process and never fully commit to one. The biggest issue is the lack of a fully formed idea. After all, it is hard to know where to start visioning in a world with endless possibilities. However, creation of the vision is the single most important step and it is imperative you focus on developing it—and developing it first.

Since everyone's vision is distinct, I can't tell you whether to turn left or right at the crossroad. However, I can give you some insight as to how you'll know when you have truly found that vision. I've created different visions throughout my life and continue to do so. For me, it is a way of living. I start defining my vision by what excites me, what truly motivates me. I'm one of the lucky people who don't find the visioning process difficult. I love it, actually. It gives me the opportunity to fully open my heart and mind and free my brain to consider any possibility.

As I work my way through the visioning process, I literally need to <u>see</u> the vision in my mind. My approach relies on a 360-degree, crystal ball-type mindset where you can rotate your point of view and see every aspect and angle of what you are trying to achieve. I visualize my starting point, every major milestone along the journey, and most importantly the successful outcome of my perfect little vision.

This process will take time. Commit to giving yourself the time and patience needed to fully develop and explore your vision. Visualize your goal until it is so clear in your mind that you can succinctly articulate it. If you can't succinctly articulate it, you're not finished with the visioning process. Also, if the vision is not crystal clear to you, the outcome will likely not be what was intended. Similarly, if you find your vision in a continual state of change, that too will negatively affect the outcome.

There are three subcomponents that need to be explored during your journey to identify a complete, 360-degree vision:

- Type of vision
- Self-reflection
- Importance and motivation behind achieving the vision (to you personally or your team)

Determining Your Type of Vision

In my experience, there are three different types of visions—personal, career-focused, and business-driven. Each is distinctly different and contains varying dynamics, roles, and responsibilities. A personal vision is just as the name suggests. It is a vision that is personal to an individual and for the most part a single person has primary responsibility for achieving the vision. It is my opinion that everyone should have personal visions throughout their lifetime. It keeps our minds fresh and continually motivated toward achieving something positive. Personal visions can range from running a marathon to learning a new language or contributing to your community.

The second type of vision is a career-focused vision. Whether you are an athlete or an employee in a company, it is wise to have a vision of how you will grow and advance your career over the next five years. If you don't have a vision for your career, I can almost guarantee you will retire doing exactly what you are doing today. Give yourself the opportunity to achieve more by creating your career vision. Again, this type of vision relies primarily on a single source of accountability (you!), but also a support network of implementers, which we will discuss later in this chapter.

The third type of vision is business-driven. These visions are typically held by business owners, team leaders, or CEOs who are responsible for creating a vision for a team of people. This type of vision is the most complex and contains different layers of management and varying roles and responsibilities. Business-driven visions are the foundation of successful companies. They must be very well defined, succinctly articulated to the team, and have clear lines of authority and accountability.

Self-reflection

Take some time to reflect on your own self to identify who you think you are and why you exist. Be honest with yourself. Are you willing to do whatever it takes, or are there certain guidelines you will adhere to in order to preserve your character? The answers to those questions create the fabric of your being and act as your moral compass. This is important, because as you work through the details of your vision, you may have to make some difficult choices. Knowing who you are and why you exist will guide your decisions and actions away from things you know in your heart that you are unwilling to compromise to achieve any vision.

For obvious reasons, it is much easier to understand the how and why of existence for an individual than it is for a business or a team. However, if you are defining the character of a business or leading a team working toward a common goal, you will need to consider a more complex definition. A shared vision, the dynamics of the individuals within the team, and what motivates them all need to be explored to build a solid foundation for your vision.

Identify the Importance of Your Vision

Similarly, understanding the importance and motivation behind your vision is essential. Begin by asking yourself a few questions:

- Why is this vision important to me personally?
- How strong do I feel about the vision I'm creating?
- Am I willing to do whatever it takes to achieve this vision?
- If I don't achieve this vision, how will it affect me personally? (e.g. is my vision a "nice to have" or an absolute "must have")

You already know that achieving your vision is going to be hard work—very hard work. It is going to take time, and effort, and in many cases the support of others. So, without an unyielding commitment to your vision, you are wasting your time. Personal commitment sets your metaphorical compass and is the first step to success.

Once you have developed a vision that is clear in your mind and you can articulate it effectively, you are ready to begin Step 2—defining your vision and the expected outcomes.

Step 2: Define the Vision and Expected Outcomes

Now that we've finished the creative, self-reflecting visioning process, it is time to define some goals to measure our progress and accomplishments. Any vision is attainable when you define it in a series of steps or actions that inch you toward your end goal.

Begin by creating a timeline for your vision. It can range from a couple weeks to several years, depending on your individual vision. Ensure the timeline is reasonable and attainable based on the complexity of your vision and how much time you will devote on a daily basis. If you aspire to unreasonable expectations, you will get discouraged and likely quit before you reach your vision.

Next, break your vision down into bite-size actions that are the building blocks of the whole. You can adjust these interim goals and actions as necessary along the way, but make sure each is clearly defined and measurable. If you find you're blowing your goals off the map, don't be afraid to accelerate your timeline and work harder. Write your goals down and hold yourself accountable to achieving them. Literally write down each individual action (along with additional details if it is complex), the timeframe for completion, and a quantifiable result that serves as proof of your accomplishment. This is especially important if you are working in a team setting. People like to feel they are achievers and winners, so create a plan using George T. Doran's "SMART" (Specific, Measurable, Attainable, Relative, Time-bound) objectives. This creates an environment of acceptance and accountability toward individual actions.

Step 3: Visualize Success of Your End Game

Successful people harness the power of visualization to their advantage. It is a very powerful yet simple process. Sit down, close your eyes, and create a mental picture of what it looks like when you've obtained your vision. Ask yourself how you will feel when you achieve your vision and what that physically looks like. This powerful exercise provides the clarity for you to move forward with motivation and excitement as you continue to complete the detailed actions you created in Step 2.

The Change[11]

The visualization process is so powerful that it isn't surprising that many athletes use it to achieve success. Olympians can literally see themselves on the podium after a competition—heart pounding, gold medal heavy around their neck, and smiling to the tune of their national anthem. Visualization is the tool used to foster that type of dedication and passion, year after year.

I first learned the power of visualization from my dive coach in college. I was a diver on the swim team and coach would teach me new dives (ones I had never attempted) by visualizing and feeling the correct way to execute the dive. I could see myself doing the dive, breaking down the different steps in my mind: high step; hand up; head back; knees to chest; straighten legs; cross hands; enter water; and then wait for the perfect 10 from the judges. Ok, so I never got a perfect 10, but by visualizing exactly what my body was doing and feeling, I felt in control and confident. It allowed me to put any fear aside, keep moving forward, and continually improve.

Another benefit to visualizing your end game is that it can actually help solidify your plan. Creating that image in your mind makes it somewhat real and no longer a dream. One of my favorite visions, which my family can attest to, was my determination to be a contestant on the reality TV series *Survivor*. I had been a devoted viewer and fan of the show since it first aired and I told my family on numerous occasions that the show was made for me. I needed to get on that show. Yes, me and millions of others, but I knew they didn't want it as badly as I did. So, as my kids grew up, I began to send in audition tapes. It wasn't pretty, but after four years and countless videos, I finally got the call I'd been determined to get. Survivor was calling! The point to this story is that I spent four years visualizing myself at the final tribal council, complete with the speech I would deliver to the tribal jury. Ultimately, I did make it to the final tribal council, but was not given the opportunity to deliver my final speech. However, my detailed planning, visualization, and commitment were absolutely instrumental in bringing my vision to life. As long as you can see the possibilities around you, you can find a way to achieve them.

Now, you have to sell your vision to others. I use the word "sell" because that is exactly what you must do and I don't think many people think of it that way. But, if your success depends on support from others (in whole or in part), you have to sell your passion, excitement, and motivation. Whether you are leading a team or are simply relying on the support of friends and family, you need to present them with the details of your vision in a way that shows your passion and excitement. If you can do that successfully, they will be as passionate and motivated as you are.

Step 4: Communicate the Vision with Passion and Energy

Steps 4 and 5 go hand-in-hand with each other. You must be able to communicate the vision with passion and energy, and by doing so you will effectively build a movement of inspired implementers (Step 5).

Let's start with the concept of communicating with passion and energy. You must be able to show others how and why your vision is so important, and ensure that they can see the vision in the same light and matter of importance as you do. However, this is not about being a cheerleader. It is more than that. It is about getting people to believe in the vision, to feel bound and committed to the vision in much the same way that you are. This is an important step, so don't take it lightly. Often times, people skip this step completely and move forward with no buy-in from individuals that may be instrumental to success. Take some time to think about who those people are, what you need from them, and what will happen if you aren't able to effectively articulate your vision. As a second step, take the time and put in the effort to perfect your message. Time is short and people are often quick to make a decision based on the first few minutes (or even seconds) of your interaction. You will have a very small window of time to gain buy-in to something that is very important to you—make those minutes count by being prepared. Be clear and be succinct in your message.

This topic reminds me of the TV show *Shark Tank* where entrepreneurs seeking money have only minutes to gain the support

The Change[11]

of one of the Sharks (Millionaires ready to invest in their business) or they will leave with nothing. The contestants must be prepared and think through the types of questions that the "Sharks" will ask in advance. In order to win, they have to sell themselves as much, if not more, than they sell their products or services. The winners are enthusiastic, high-energy personalities set upon achieving their goals. Use these same tactics when you communicate your vision. The more you believe in your vision, the better prepared you are; the better prepared you are, the better you sell the vision; the better you sell the vision, the greater the chance you have at gaining support and achieving it.

If you are a gifted seller and communicator, others will even go so far as to provide you with ideas on how they can help. When this happens, you know you have inspired them and they are a valued member of your support team. These people are the ones you will count on to move the vision forward, day-by-day, creating a movement toward the future. Congratulations! You have built the movement and these individuals are your inspired implementers!

Step 5: Build a Movement of Inspired Implementers

As you begin to build this movement, the key to success is to select the right people to help you along the way—your inspired implementers. Your goal is to actually find clones of yourself! Well, not really, but you get the point. You need people that have the same level of commitment and excitement you do. If not for your actual vision, for your ultimate success. Depending on the complexity of your vision, these implementers can be all types of people and have roles of varying significance. For example, if my personal vision is to get fit, an implementer could be the neighbor who watches my kids while I exercise, a friend who commits to exercise with me and hold me accountable, or a spouse that throws out all my junk food. I like to think of these people as enablers and supporters. They may not be fully committed to my <u>vision</u> (because it is a personal vision), but they are fully committed to helping me <u>achieve</u> my vision. If you are working in a team environment, the roles, requirements, and organizational structure of the implementers is much more formal and defined. In these cases, the team implementers must maintain a specific skill set that contributes toward the vision. For these roles, you must identify successful, credible, flexible implementers who have the ability to communicate effectively with others.

You now have the tools to identify, define, and implement your vision. Are you ready to get started?

***

Carolyn J. Rivera

President

CJR Leadership Strategies

"Ignite Your Will To Win"

813-643-4414

www.carolynjrivera.com

https://www.facebook.com/carolynjrivera/

https://www.linkedin.com/in/carolyn-rivera-9b7469b?trk=hp-identity-name

https://twitter.com/Cjrleadership

Michael Cole

I was born in New Haven, Connecticut in 1962. My parents were immigrants from Jamaica. My father was born in St. Elizabeth and my mother was from the city of Kingston. My father immigrated to America to study to become a minister. He later sent for my mother in Jamaica to come to America. My parents left Kansas City and moved to New Haven, Connecticut. My father is now retired; however, he started one of the largest Jamaican American churches in the Bronx—Bronx Bethany Church of the Nazarene. I received my introduction to entrepreneurship while answering a card that had an 800 number on it. I listened to the recorded message and later got started in that business. Though it was difficult at first, I was hooked on being an entrepreneur. I have since met many successful people who taught me not only sales skills, but spirituality, psychology, and quantum physics. I was introduced to neuro-linguistic programming by a coach who taught us how to use it on the telephone. I am currently an advance speaker in Toastmasters in NYC District 46. My club members are instrumental in my success as a speaker.

How to Get Anything You Want by Using the Magic of NLP

By Michael Cole

My intention in writing this chapter is to provide you with a beginner's manual on the little known science of Neuro-linguistic Programming (NLP). NLP has the capacity to improve your life by enhancing your communications skills and by changing the way you think and perceive the world around you. I am going to take you on a journey. Together, we'll discover how far down "the rabbit hole" goes. Ultimately, you'll experience more happiness and confidence.

As in the movie *The Matrix*, you have the choice of taking the proverbial "blue pill" and go back to the life that you know. Or you can take the "red pill" and practice the skills of NLP and change your life.

John Grandier and Richard Bandler created NLP in the 1970s. *Neuro* refers to the mind or nervous system. *Linguistic* denotes language used to "rewire" the mind. Our subconscious is a powerful tool that functions like radar, scanning its environment. With NLP, we are communicating with the unconscious mind, which is where 96 percent of decisions are made. Your unconscious mind can process up to 800 times faster than your conscious mind.

How I learned about NLP

One day, my coach and I were on the phone with a leader in our industry. Following the conversation, my coach said to me, "Mike, your energy is low." At that point, I realized that something was missing from my life, and I began searching for the missing link.

My introduction into NLP came when I started a home-based business. I was working with a communications company. I became frustrated because I wasn't making sales. I wasn't alone. The sales team complained that they were exhausting their personal lists of prospects and referrals.

So the company hired a consultant. The consultant recommended a phone sales specialist. He was one of the consultant's top students. The specialist had paid Tony Robbins, NLP master trainer and famous motivational speaker, $10,000 to teach him NLP. The specialist could predictably sponsor 3 to 5 people a week using Robbins' system. All the training was done online.

Mirroring and Matching

One of the first techniques taught to our sales team by the specialist was mirroring and matching. This technique was created by Dr. Milton Erickson, a genius hypnotherapist. Dr. Erickson was one of three people John Grandier and Richard Bandler modeled. Ericksonian hypnosis uses conversation to effect change in an individual. Grandier and Bandler also modeled Fritz Peris and Virginia Satir.

As we spoke on the phone to our prospects, we mirrored and matched their tone, tempo, and volume. By doing this, we built rapport with our prospects.

People buy from people who they know, like, and trust. During our interview, we looked for clues that allowed us to establish a common bond. When the prospect answered our call, we would typically say, "Hi John, how are you?" This technique suggested to our prospect that we knew them already. We worked from a script. If our prospect said he or she had small children, we would say we did too, if that was true, or we could mention someone we knew who did have such children.

We learned to recognize personality types, conduct critical thinking, and develop sensory acuity. Critical thinking is an important business skill. We were looking for people who understood how to raise or borrow the capital needed to start a business or launch a project. Most of today's millionaires and billionaires acquired such capital.

Sensory acuity is the ability to be present in the moment and to notice what is going on in the surrounding area. For example, if while talking to a prospect we overheard a baby crying in the background, we would bring that to the attention of our prospect to build rapport.

The most challenging skill for me to learn was how to be "in state." It's your state of being; it's energy. It has its roots in quantum physics. People can feel your energy. When you're around people, you want to convey an exciting, confident, and attractive energy. They are attracted to these qualities.

Our coach recommended that we talk standing up. This conveys more energy to our prospects, who hear it in our voices. I found that, after much practice, my skills improved. I made more sales and enrolled more people. I became comfortable talking on the phone to strangers.

When mirroring and matching in person, one should seek to match the prospect's posture, hand gestures, breathing, tone, tempo, and volume. Seven percent of communication is verbal. But 38 percent is tone, and 55 percent is physiology. The unconscious mind processes information much faster than the conscious mind and is responsible for nearly all our decision making.

Pacing and leading

Mirroring and matching should be subtle. Look carefully at what hand gestures and stance the prospect is using. Wait six seconds, and then mirror their movement.

There are many tools in the NLP kit. You can mirror a bad stance or low tone and at the same time use language designed to pace the conversation and to lead the prospect out of a bad stance.

Successful pacing and leading can result in developing such rapport that your prospect begins to mirror you. For example, you're at a table with someone and you reach for your drinking glass. Then your prospect reaches for his glass and takes a sip. He is now pacing you. In making sales, such rapport is powerful.

NLP takes practice to master, but when you do, you have the power to influence and to improve people's lives.

Practice, practice, practice

Our instructor implored us to practice. So I went out and about to networking events. I focused on hand gestures and posture. Then I focused on the tone, tempo, and speech volume. Recently, at an event, I spoke with two men and a woman. I noticed that the woman and I were in such rapport that one of the men abruptly walked away. However, I did feel as if I was improving.

Sub-modalities

The next NLP technique we learned was sub-modalities. It is based on the VAKOG system. V-visual, A-auditory, K-kinesthetic, O-olfactory, and G-gustatory. People have a preference when it comes to receiving new information. They tend to be visual, auditory (listening or sound), or kinesthetic (feelings). For example, if a person is visual, you may ask them, "do you see what I mean?" If they're auditory, you may say, "how does that sound to you?" If they're kinesthetic, you may ask, "how does that make you feel?"

How do you know which modality someone prefers? You listen to his or her language. That will give you clues. Also notice the eyes. Often if the person looks up, he's visual. If she's looking straight, she's auditory. And if he's looking down, it's a clue that he's kinesthetic. Watch your favorite talk show or news broadcast and notice what people are saying or doing with their eyes.

Anchoring

Anchoring is intentionally using gestures or touch to elicit a desired feeling. Anchoring is used to modify a feeling or emotion by inserting a trigger. We want to replace a negative trigger with a positive trigger. One technique we learned to prompt feelings of confidence involved clenching our hands into fists and closing our eyes. We thought of a time when we felt confident. That created a trigger. So every time we felt less than confident, we clinched our hands and that would trigger a time when we were confident. That exercise helped us to anchor a feeling of confidence that would replace any anxiety we may have felt.

The Meta Model

The Meta Model is designed to change the way that we think. It is a problem-solving modality. It is based on presuppositions. In other words, our brain will drop whatever information that fails to match a current pattern in our thinking. The presuppositions that we are concerned about are the ones that limit our expectations such as, "I can't sell" or "I can't do public speaking." Most presuppositions are based on events that happened in the past.

However, we can challenge these presuppositions. Sometimes we can make them disappear altogether. We can do this by challenging the linguistics and the entire idea of the presupposition.

By asking our prospect a series of questions, we can discover her frame of reference. In NLP, it's called a "map" or "model of the world." Then we use the "framing tool," which is a series of questions designed to take the client to the edge of their map. If you change that frame, you can change the mental picture in the frame. Techniques such as these turned a shy person like me, who felt like a failure and had trouble making sales, into someone who now feels better and shows improvement in many areas of his life. I feel more comfortable and confident socially and in business. My relationships have also improved. I started attending Toastmasters meetings in New York City to learn public speaking. Public speaking has been cited as one of the most feared skills. Speaking publicly was not a skill I would have attempted 5 years ago. However, because of learning NLP and with the help of Toastmasters, I was able to overcome my fears and speak in front of groups. My relationships have improved in business as well as personally. I had a very bad case of social anxiety; however, because of learning NLP, it slowly disappeared. It is said in NLP that the map is not the territory. We live in our head, not the world. We have a map of the world. What that means is that our perceptions are not the reality.

I invite you to investigate the science of Neuro-linguistic programming. To learn more about NLP go to michaelsuccess.com.

The intention of the founders of NLP is to create excellence in human behavior, rather than manipulate people. All kinds of professions use NLP such as doctors, chiropractors, lawyers, therapists, salespeople, and entrepreneurs. NLP can result in extraordinary results and cause lasting change in the way a person communicates and thinks. Once you start to change the way you think, you will discover how to get anything you want using the magic of NLP.

***

To contact Michael:

michaelsuccess.com

http://michaelsvision.isagenix.com/?sc_lang=en-US

914-290-1540

mikecole62@gmail.com

Gina Gardiner

Gina Gardiner is an inspirational speaker, NLP Master Practitioner, coach, trainer, and mentor specializing in personal empowerment and transformational leadership. She is described by Ofsted as an "Inspirational leader" and as an "Impressive coach and exceptional mentor" by Investors in People.

Gina used her experience of running an award-winning school from a wheelchair and learning to walk twice as an adult to develop a unique point of view and a different approach to leadership and living an empowered life. Gina has since helped countless clients live a happier, more confident, loving and fulfilled life.

Her books include *Chariots On Fire*, *Kick Start Your Career*, and *How You Can Manage Your Staff More Effectively*.

Created out of necessity, her approach has proven that once you start to change how you think, you start to change your reality and that of those around you. Her powerful strategies are underpinned by the belief that it's not the challenges which define us but how we deal with them.

Her powerful yet practical approach could help you realize you are enough! You too can live a truly happy and fulfilled life and enjoy great relationships when you are being genuinely you.

It's Your Choice!

Genuinely You

Discover how to live a happy, confident, and stress free life starting today!

By Gina Gardiner

"If you always do what you have always done you will always get what you already have." Albert Einstein

It may sound clichéd but it remains the absolute truth. Life is about choice, the quality of your choices absolutely determine the quality of your life. Everything you do is a choice. What you do and how you do it is up to you. The words you say, their tone, and the timing are yours to decide. Just as importantly, it is your choice to do nothing or to say silent.

Moment by moment we have the opportunity to choose how we think and act or to allow unconscious patterns of thinking to determine the quality of our lives. Every choice we make has consequences. Failing to choose is in reality a choice, the consequences of which can be both significant and far reaching.

It is your choice whether you listen to the voice telling you that you are not good enough because you are too young or too old, or you don't have enough time, money, experience, or nerve to do something. There are always lots of reasons why something won't work. It is also your choice to focus on what you can do, to be brave, and to try new things. True empowerment is about being prepared to face your fear and get on with it. It is in the small daily acts that your courage, compassion, and true power will shine through.

The amazing thing is that when you let go of negativity and believe in yourself, magic begins to happen! As the author of your own life story, give yourself the star role as the hero rather than the victim. From today, choose to make active, informed choices.

When you read this you may think to yourself "It's all right for her, she hasn't had to deal with all the challenges I've faced" and that is true. However, I speak from the experience of someone who has faced physical difficulties since a serious ski accident in 1983. I've learned to walk twice as an adult and understand the daily struggle of living with long-term pain and disability.

I believe that it is not the challenges which define us but how we deal with them. It is when life gets difficult that we have the greatest opportunity to learn and grow and within that there is an amazing gift—if you look for it.

Be Mindful

Many people have destroyed every chance of succeeding before they get started. If you believe you will fail, the chances are you will. Be fearful of failure and the decisions you make will be based on that fear. Those decisions will sabotage your chances of succeeding.

Look at how consistently successful people approach life and you will find a common pattern of thinking based on the belief 'I will succeed.' They have faith that whatever happens, they will find a way to achieve their goals. They see failure is an opportunity to learn and grow and have the persistence to keep going until they achieve success. Do they have superhuman attributes? I don't believe so. We all have that capacity if we choose to believe in ourselves.

Think of a baby learning to walk—failure is not an option. No matter how many times they fall, they keep going. Consider how different life would be if you had maintained that same level of faith and commitment.

The Power of Belief

Research shows that 95% of our thoughts are habitual and based on our beliefs. Our early experiences shape our beliefs and we then use them to interpret everything. We consistently look for evidence to support the view that our beliefs are right.

Imagine two people in a park—they see the same dog. One is frightened, as she was bitten as a child. The dog approaches, she screams, and the dog growls. The other remembers her favourite pet and greets the dog with confidence; the dog wags its tail. It's the same dog, but people use their experience to confirm that their beliefs about dogs are correct.

Challenging the beliefs which limit us is important. Until Roger Banister ran the 4-minute mile, no one thought it possible, yet within a month of his achieving it, over 30 others had done the same.

Several years ago, I attended a fantastic course in London—Unleash The Power Within (UPW). I wanted to attend another course offered by Tony Robbins, but had dismissed it because it was in California. How would I manage by myself in the wheelchair? I thought it was just too difficult.

UPW involved a Fire Walk. My mobility was limited to a few steps, but with help I succeeded. I was ecstatic! I turned to watch the next guy—a double amputee who walked over the burning coals on his hands. I was gobsmacked!

In that moment, I asked myself; if he could do that, how often did I self-limit? I immediately booked the course in America. I travelled on my own and had a fabulous time. Since then I've travelled abroad on my own to study and to speak many times. I'm so grateful to that nameless man who challenged the quality of my thinking.

How often do you choose to limit yourself because of your beliefs?

Changing Perceptions and Motives

It is just as important to challenge your perceptions and the meaning you make about the motives of others. Things are not always what you think.

Imagine you are driving when someone behind you keeps tailgating and trying to get past you. What is your immediate reaction? Do you get irritated, thinking "What a jerk"?

What if you knew that the driver had just received a phone call from the hospital saying their child had been badly injured and was about to go into surgery?

How about the person who blames their parents for their lack of confidence because they never seemed satisfied and were always criticizing? Was their motive created out of wanting to make their child unhappy or in a desire for them to be the best they could be?

By blaming the parents, this person takes no responsibility for themselves. Until they do, they will be stuck in the role of victim.
In my experience, most parents want the best for their children. Understanding that their parents were doing the best they could with the resources they had available and forgiving them for any hurt gives them the freedom to let go of the past; by doing so, the quality of their present and future will be vastly improved.

When we hand the responsibility for how we feel to others, we give away our power.

No one can make you happy or angry unless you let them.

Learn to Use Your Resources Wisely

Time, energy, and money are finite resources. Faith, love, and gratitude are just three of the infinite resources available to us all.

The Bible describes a lifespan as 3 score years and ten.

70 years is 25,567 ½ days or 613,620 hours.

How do you spend yours?

Do you waste time worrying, moaning, feeling guilty, regretting, or looking backwards? Is there a better way to use such a precious commodity?

The only time we can guarantee is this moment. Moment by moment, are you making the most of yours?

Imagine living out your life just as you do now. Think about the legacy you will leave behind. Will you have any regrets? Think about the relationships you have sustained in your life time and how people will describe you at your funeral. Will you have achieved your life's true purpose?

It is your choice to stay just as you are or to make the changes which will make the difference.

Your energy can only be used once. Many things drain your energy: incompletions, stress, unhappiness, poor health, being unfulfilled. How well do you look after yourself? Do you eat healthily and sleep well? Do you choose to be happy? Research demonstrates that not only are happy people healthier, but they are also more creative, productive, and better at problem solving.

If you are stressed or in overwhelm, what help can you draw upon? Getting expert help makes sense.

Money is a form of energy. We can use money to buy other people's time and expertise.

The relationship you have with money determines how healthy your bank balance is. In my experience, those who struggle with money have very negative beliefs about money and they constantly focus on the fear of not having enough. Their beliefs around deserving and lack have often spanned several generations. Transforming the situation requires a shift in both beliefs and behaviors around money. Reassuringly, once there is a positive change in the relationship people have with money, things improve significantly.

Many of us are too busy being a human doing rather than a human being. In the hubbub of daily living, it is easy to lose sight of the amazing spiritual resources available to us.

- *Having faith in yourself as a powerful, talented, creative, loving being*
- *Appreciating the abundant Universe*
- *Knowing that with failure comes greater understanding and the opportunity to learn and grow—so long as you keep going*
- *Trusting you have the strength to deal with everything life brings, however challenging*
- *Being generous of spirit and knowing you will receive in kind*

- *Knowing that by living in love you achieve so much more than living in fear*
- *Being grateful for the wonder each day offers and for the people you love*

Meditation, enjoying nature, or simply being still and quiet on a regular basis will help you access them.

These resources enable us to live a truly abundant and amazing life. It is your choice whether you give yourself permission to receive and enjoy these gifts. They are yours for the asking.

You Get More of What You Focus on—Choose Wisely

There is a strong relationship between where our energy and focus are placed and what we manifest. When you focus your thoughts and your energy on the negative things in life, they appear to take on an ever greater significance and the sense of fear and lack grows stronger. This leeches energy and leads to a sense of hopelessness and overwhelm.

Focus on what you want more of in your life and the same principle holds true.

Becoming wheelchair bound was a significant challenge for me. When I first came out of hospital following surgery, I couldn't stand, manage a shower, or go out of the house by myself. If my morning caregiver had not left a cup and filled the kettle for me, I couldn't make myself a drink. It would have been very easy to focus on all the things I couldn't do. I had my brain, my hands, and my mouth. In fact, I had everything I needed to run my school effectively. By choosing to focus on what I could do, I enjoyed a far better quality of life and achieved something really worthwhile.

Be Loving

The most important relationship is the one you have with yourself. You are the common denominator throughout your life. Every relationship is colored by the way you think about and treat yourself.

The Change[11]

Many of my clients wonder why they can't find true love. They have been treated badly by a succession of partners and are very unhappy. Others are looking for someone else to sort out their lives, to organize and take care of them. They are disappointed when the partners they choose fail to make the difference.

Time and time again, I find that those same clients have a terrible relationship with themselves. They feel worthless. When asked to identify what they don't like about themselves, the list is endless. When asked what they like, they struggle to find much to say.

Ask yourself do you treat your best friend in the same way as you treat yourself? Are your expectations the same for you as they are for them? If they mess up, do you forgive easily? When you mess up, does the voice in your head go on endlessly telling you off? How would your life be different if you started to treat yourself as a well-loved and valued friend?

You are enough just as you are! Appreciate what an amazing, creative, talented, unique person you are. You have the capacity to be powerful and loving. When you believe in yourself, life becomes full of possibilities.

Be Forgiving

Holding a grudge is like giving yourself the poison and expecting the other person to feel the pain. It does nothing to punish them or hold them to account. It hurts only you. Whilst you hold on to the negative feelings about them, there is an inextricable chain which binds you to them and removes any power to move on.

Forgiving does not mean you have to condone the action which has caused so much grief. Nor does it mean forgetting. Forgiving gives you the gift of freedom.

A client came to see me because she was struggling with OCD. We looked at the underlying cause. She disclosed that she had been abused over a long period by her grandfather. Through our work she was able to forgive the man who had caused her so much distress.

She was finally able to start healing and leave the past behind her. It allowed her to change the patterns of obsessive behavior which had been destroying the quality of her and her family's life. She recognized the strength and resilience developed through her challenges. She is now happy and doing well.

Be Grateful

I believe gratitude has the capacity to change lives hugely for the better. We are so lucky to live in such a beautiful world, yet so many of us take it for granted. If you are reading this book, chances are you are one of the most privileged people on this planet. You have enough to eat, decent plumbing with clean water, and medical support available if needed.

Take the time to notice the small things you are grateful for during every day. Before you go to sleep, scan the day and choose 5 things to put on your gratitude list. Doing so will focus your mind on the positive rather than on all the irritations which daily living offers. Time and time again, I've watched how completing this simple activity regularly for a month has a dramatic and positive effect on the way clients think and feel about themselves.

Look For The Gift

Within every challenge lies a gift. Six months after the accident, I became the Principal of a large school. Deteriorating mobility and two failed back surgeries left me using a wheelchair full time. My challenge was how to ensure excellence for pupils and staff despite not being able to get through the doorways.

The old saying that "necessity is the mother of invention" was never truer; over time, I developed a structured, sequential professional staff development program which involved all staff. Living proof of its success was our inclusion on the HMI "Best 100 Schools" list twice during my headship.

The gifts of my disability have been significant. They include the highly successful approach I created for developing empowered leaders and the strategies I developed, initially to help myself. These strategies have since helped hundreds of clients. You can find them and share more of my journey in *Chariots On Fire*.

Live Your True Purpose

I have met many clients who on paper have all the outward trappings of success, and yet feel empty and unhappy. Whilst they come for very different reasons, at the heart of the matter lies a very similar issue. They have a successful career or business, earn lots of money, and have all the things affluence brings, but deep down they are unfulfilled because they are not following their true purpose.

Choosing to live your true purpose offers you the opportunity to experience a lasting and deep sense of passion and fulfilment. It makes your heart sing. It comes when you know you are making a positive difference in the world.

Find Genuine Fulfilment

Being fulfilled comes from being genuinely, authentically you. From learning to love who you are now, warts and wobbly bits too. It comes from holding oneself accountable and aiming to become the best you can be. It's about looking for the lesson when we make a mistake so we don't make the same mistake again and in looking for the gifts that come within life's challenges.

It comes from being curious about the world and how it works, from learning from others past and present. By being open to the possibilities that present themselves and the learning that those possibilities offer. It's about using failing as an opportunity to develop and grow.

Fulfilment is about contribution and service to others. Giving selflessly with no wish for personal gain offers the potential for the greatest fulfilment. Try making random acts of kindness to complete strangers, without any need for recognition or acknowledgement. There is fulfilment in realizing there is no such thing as separation. We are all children of God.

You can choose to find fulfilment in your everyday life or look for the irritations and difficulties. Either way, you will find what you are looking for. Everything has the potential to be extraordinary. From the moment you open your eyes, choose to be happy and notice the wonder each moment offers. Make the most of every relationship and live every day as if it were your last.

Take the time to notice all the things that nurture your spirit and tackle anything in your life that gets in the way of you living your life to the full.

Every day is precious—if you would like help making the most of yours, I'd be delighted to help.

***

To contact Gina:

+44(0)1206 230497

Skype: gina.gardiner2

Email: gina@genuinelygina.co.uk

Website: www.GenuinelyGina.co.uk/Change

(Download a free Life Audit Tool)

Facebook: https://www.facebook.com/genuinelygina/

Linkedin: https://www.uk.linkedin.com/in/ginagardinerassociates

Joy Humbarger

Joy Humbarger is the Founder and CEO of Maximize Your Leadership, a business dedicated to helping managers at all levels leverage their skills and that of their employees. With more than 30 years of professional experience in education and leadership instruction, Joy has trained more than 8,000 leaders around the world, and has supported more than 700 leaders in one-to-one coaching settings. She works to shift mindsets from negativity and conflict to positive, productive, solutions-based thinking.

Joy has a passion for helping each person discover and celebrate their own unique strengths, as well as the strengths of others. She is dedicated to providing processes that use open, two-way communication and positive change.

Joy received her B.S. in Business and Psychology and an M.S. in Early Childhood Education. She is a Professional Certified Leadership Coach (PCC) and received her Energy Leadership Index Assessment – Master Practitioner Certification (ELI-MP) in 2014.

When she's not supporting others to grow, you can find Joy curled up in a chair reading mysteries, beating her husband at Rummy, or playing with her active and ornery grandsons.

Leading the F____!! Out of Change

Joy Humbarger

As the new changes were announced about the company's upcoming acquisition, I looked around the room at the faces of the employees. Their reactions would determine the work Jess, their leader, and I (Jess's coach) would do to help them navigate what was coming.

There was grumbling, blaming, crying, and even some hesitant enthusiasm. After working with leaders for many years, this was an all too familiar scene for me. The change was not only a surprise to her employees, but also to Jess. In addition to dealing with fallout from employees, she would also have to work through her own feelings about the change.

Our work was cut out for us. Jess and I knew that in the coming months we would be dealing with everything from excitement to anger, hesitation, duplicity, and grief. She would have to lead the F(ear)!! out of change.

We are all leaders in some area of our life, whether we choose to be or not. And we all experience change. Change can be anything from a merger or company acquisition, to a change in leadership, processes, your role in the company, or even something as simple as having a new copier and the frustration of not being able to make copies quickly. It can also be a change in your personal world: an unexpected illness or a child going off to college.

Reflection

Think about your own experience with a change you weren't ready for but had to cope with anyway.

What were you were feeling at that time?

If you were resistant to that change, what created that resistance?

What words did you use to describe how you were feeling?

See Change Through Their Eyes

Jess and I worked together to help her understand how to effectively handle the various reactions of her employees as they navigated the coming changes. We started by defining change to help Jess understand the mindset of her team. According to *Merriam-Webster Dictionary*, change is "a modification to one's environment, situation, or physical/mental condition that results in a challenge to one's existing beliefs of how their world is supposed to work."

This change represented a huge shift in employee beliefs about what their work was, how it should be done, and how new people would impact the processes and space. We began creating a running list of questions her team might have. This would help her prepare answers and create thought-provoking questions for her team, encouraging them all to co-create the new workplace culture. Below are the initial questions she thought would be asked:

Why weren't we consulted about what was going to happen?

Why are the new people moving into this space?

What adjustments will I have to make to my workspace to accommodate them?

What will happen to me if there are too many employees now? Will I lose my job?

How will our current processes change?

Has this or something similar ever happened in your personal or professional life? Change creates of lot of uncertainty. What we don't know tends to scare us. As a result, we may act pretty irrationally to try to prevent change, often without realizing it. We can make our lives and the lives of others unnecessarily problematic.

Where does all this fear come from? When we are born, we have no beliefs or values. As we grow, we are influenced by many factors including our families, our neighborhood, our community, our experiences, our education, and a host of other things. Over time, we develop core beliefs and values that make up our paradigm for how life is supposed to be. They become the perception, or lens, through which we view the world.

As an example, you may have always spent the holidays with particular family members on a particular day. As families grow and change, that "tradition" changes. It can be hard to accept new family members and their traditions. And if you go to someone else's house for the holiday, it never feels the same as being at home with your own traditions.

Changing the way you do things is hard, harder yet when you've been doing them for a long time. As we age, we encounter more difficulties processing changes because our paradigms, or beliefs, values, and expectations, are more ingrained. We tend to find friends and form groups that reinforce our beliefs. When many people agree, it's easy to discount the differing opinions of others, even if the others have undeniable logic. So, we attack the possibility of change because we think we know better than everyone else and have the friends to back us up.

Reflection

What habits or beliefs do you have that would be difficult to change?

How would you feel if someone told you to change those patterns?

What is the absolute worst thing you think could happen if you changed your status quo?

How likely is it that the worst thing will happen?

Meet Basic Human Needs

Fear is a key factor in resistance to change. It raises its ugly head because our basic human needs are not being met. This can happen with changes we decide to make on our own, but it is most prevalent when changes are thrust upon us.

As Jess and I reviewed the seven basic human needs, we added some questions to her list. These would help her become more aware of which needs were not being met, and how to address them.

<u>Safe</u>: We need to feel safe physically, mentally, emotionally, and in our relationships.

How will this change affect my job? My home life?

What will happen if I don't know how to make the changes?

What will happen if I make mistakes?

What if it takes me longer to learn than others?

What if I don't understand what is expected of me?

<u>Seen</u>: Each of us needs to know that we are valued for who we are, and for our work. Feedback, or what I call "feed forward," is intended to support growth. It is an important component in meeting the need to be seen.

What do you know about me?

What do you notice about my work or the things I do to enhance our family?

How valuable do you think my actions are to the company? Our relationship?

<u>Heard</u>: We need to know that we have a voice and will be listened to, even if our ideas are not necessarily used. We also need a sounding board for fears, concerns and anxieties. This helps minimize over-reaction and emotional chaos.

Will you really listen to the thoughts, ideas, and concerns I have?

<u>Respected</u>: When people feel respected, they have a stronger sense of usefulness and become a positive contributor to the change.

Will you respect me, and my experiences and knowledge?

Will you see me as a valuable member of this family, relationship, team, or organization no matter what?

<u>Connected</u>: The more people feel connected to information, people, solutions, and outcomes, the easier it is for them to embrace and contribute to the change process.

Will I be in the 'information loop' so I can understand what's coming and prepare for what I need to do?

In what other ways can I be connected in this change?

<u>Contribute</u>: When people contribute to defining, outlining steps, or creating solutions to the challenges of change, they have more buy-in and a positive attitude toward working on the change.

How can I be part of creating the steps to make this change?

How can I contribute to resolving challenges?

<u>Belong</u>: People need to be accepted by those in their workplace. They need a "tribe" they can depend on when things get tough. And, they need to see how they belong to solutions and outcomes involved in the change process.

How will I be accepted within my team or family during this change?

How will we interact together?

What role will I be expected to play?

How will I fit into all phases of this change?

Address Fears

The change had been announced. Now it was important to begin giving the team the opportunity to address the fears they might be experiencing. Jess and I reviewed the five main fears that develop around change, and how to address those fears. It was helpful for Jess to associate each fear with a quote.

Fear of **Failure:** This fear involves the need for perfection. If we don't think we can get it right, we just choose not to do anything at all. This person is feeling unsafe. There may already be an assumption that "I'm not good enough (or smart enough, or capable enough) to go through the change successfully." Fear of failure can show up through a variety of actions such as apathy, anger, or blaming. How will I be able to contribute or belong to the change? What if my experience and knowledge will not be valued in this change?

> *"When we give ourselves permission to fail, we, at the same time, give ourselves permission to excel."*
>
> ~Eloise Ristad

Fear of **Success**: This fear is about how we perceive success. We fear we might have to compromise our beliefs, becoming like someone we feel is successful but not admirable. Conquering this fear means knowing what will happen when we are successful. How will we act? What will others expect of us? How will others see and hear us? Can we handle that? Can our life be the way we want it to be? Will success change us? Will we be able to contribute and connect in the same ways?

> *"Our deepest fear is not that we are inadequate. Our deepest fear is that we are powerful beyond all measure. It is our light, not our darkness, that most frightens us. We ask ourselves, who am I to be brilliant, gorgeous, talented, and fabulous?"*
>
> ~Marianne Williamson

Fear of **Loss**: This fear focuses on what we will lose with change. Even when current circumstances are bad, at least we know what they are and how to manage them. When we invest ourselves emotionally in anything, it becomes harder to change because we don't want to lose all the time and effort we have already exerted. Perhaps we fear losing our job, the position and salary we worked so hard to achieve. Maybe we fear losing our routine, our spouse, or what we have come to know as family—things we feel define us. Will we lose the opportunity to do some of the things we love most? Will we have to give up the learned processes that make our life easier? Will we have the opportunity to be heard when we have new ideas? Will we get feedback that will help us continue to grow? Will we lose the people that are "in our corner" and support us?

> *"Don't be afraid of change. You may end up losing something good, but you will probably end up gaining something better."*
>
> ~Unknown

Fear of **Upsetting Others**: This fear is about what others think of us. Sometimes change brings positive results for one person and challenges for another. When people have worked or "lived" together for a period of time, the person who is experiencing positive results may fear that others will be upset at their good fortune. This can keep people from bettering themselves. They may be willing to refuse a promotion so they won't have to supervise their current coworkers, or deal with ill feelings from others. Someone who puts others' needs ahead of their own may become concerned that people will be upset if they are not "in it" with them because their circumstances change for the better. So, people decide not to do things, like go back to school, stop a habit, or change a tradition, because they don't want to upset others. They don't want to lose respect or the opportunity to be contributing members of the group.

> *"Stop wasting time getting upset at those who criticize your life! It's always someone who has NO IDEA of the price you paid to get to where you are today..."*
>
> ~Unknown

Fear of **Leaving a Comfort Zone**: This fear is about routines. It's difficult to face the unknown, especially when it's something we didn't create ourselves. Leaving a comfort zone can bring up a lot of self-doubt. We resist so we don't have to face our perceived potential inadequacies, the stress that comes with change, and the discomfort of finding new ways and new routines. Our brain is hardwired to identify routines and create habits. This helps us get through our days without the tremendous drain of brain energy from constantly making decisions or paying close attention. And habits allow us to focus on the things that require concentration. How long will it take to get into the new routine? When will I finally feel like I have a handle on the new ways? Can I even make this change?

> *"To the degree we're not living our dreams, our comfort zone has more control of us than we have over ourselves."*
>
> *~Peter McWilliams*

Reflection

What are some fears you have experienced?

Which of the seven basic human needs were involved in those fears?

Think about the person you identified at the beginning of this chapter who has had a difficult time with a change. What kind of fear(s) might he or she have been experiencing; and which of the basic human needs might have been involved?

What Causes Resistance to Change?

There has been a lot of research done about the reasons people resist change. Basic human needs and some form of fear are involved. Research shows that the resistance and fear center around four main reasons:

They don't know WHAT to do

They don't know HOW to do it

They don't receive feedback (feed forward)

They don't know WHY they should do it

When these reasons are addressed, people are more willing to get on board with change. This minimizes the unnecessary negativity that brings everyone's attitude down.

After Jess and I reviewed the seven basic human needs, the five fears, and the causes of resistance, Jess was prepared. She completed the list of questions, concerns, and answers she would use to guide her employees through this change.

Create CHANGE

How do leaders support others through successful, sustained change while adapting to change themselves? I shared with Jess these CHANGE steps that can be applied to both professional and personal change.

Communicate. Jess was intentional about communicating the parameters of the change, a clear framework for the outcomes, and where her team had the opportunity to be creative. She announced that she was open to all ideas about how to move forward, and encouraged her team to email her, or just stop by her office.

Harness thoughts. Our thoughts create our feelings and drive our actions, ultimately creating our results. We have a choice about how we respond to change. Once Jess understood this, she began asking people to talk about how they were feeling and what thoughts were contributing to those feelings. We encouraged each person to become more aware of their actions around the changes to better understand and harness thoughts that were not helpful. Jess also supported each person to create a new more positive, helpful mindset to approaching the situation.

Assess options. There are many right ways to move through change. At this stage, individually and as a team, we brainstormed ways the change could happen. This is an important step in moving forward and feeling in control. It represents a key turning point in mindset. Jess worked with each person to choose options for next steps that were mutually agreeable. The remaining ideas were a backup list, if needed.

Navigate strengths. It's easy for all of us to make changes when we focus on our strengths and successful past experiences, and then use those to help us move forward. Jess asked each person what they were most proud of achieving in the past, and how they could use strategies from those accomplishments to impact this change. As her team began to see connections, they also gained buy-in for making the change.

Grow skills. Jess and I also discussed possibilities for her staff to develop the new skills they would need for the change. As the leader, Jess needed to remove any barriers to progress, and provide opportunities for her staff to receive training and to mentor each other. Jess, herself, was also growing her skills as a leader as she navigated this change. A critical component of this phase is to provide "feed forward." What's going well? Where are there challenges? What options are there to resolve challenges?

Emphasize progress. Each week, Jess and I discussed where she was seeing progress in herself and her team. She also focused on progress at the beginning of team meetings, and as she met with each person individually. By focusing on progress, her team kept a positive outlook. There was less stress throughout the process, and her team was recognized for their quick adaptation to the new changes.

After working with Jess for nine months, she was ready to fly on her own. Just three months later, her team won a company award for their quick, enthusiastic response to the changes that came with the acquisition. They were instrumental in creating company-wide processes that supported full integration of new systems and personnel. Today, Jess continues to use the CHANGE formula. "Joy's formula saved us. It brought us together as a team around a situation that seemed impossible. Now, with each new initiative that comes along, we are eager to return to the formula and challenge ourselves to create the best possible solutions for change."

Being able to adapt to change takes great skill. Being able to guide others through change takes great leadership. Just as anyone can resist change, anyone can embrace change. Congratulations, Jess, for leading the F(<u>ear</u>)!! out of Change.

***

To contact Joy:

Email: Joy@MaximizeYourLeadership.com

Telephone: 913-481-4152

Website: www.MaximizeYourLeadership.com

LinkedIn: https://www.linkedin.com/in/joyhumbarger

Facebook: https://www.facebook.com/maximizeyourleadership

Renee Dean

Renee Dean is a life success coach that assists in helping people to find their purpose in life. Her concentration is mostly on educating beginners on the law of attraction. Her prior accolades include mentoring students on the Bhagavad Gita, a Hindu scripture, at Classic Insights. She was the life editor at *WE* magazine for women. She also was a host of her own radio show *Beginners Law of Attraction*. Certified in Neuro-linguistic Programming, NLP, she works with people to change patterns of behavior with subconscious reprogramming. She grew up with her father as her mentor, as he was a master hypnotist with a business in past life regressions. He shared his passions with her in quantum physics, NLP, past life regressions and almost anything metaphysical. Coming from an abusive marriage and struggling as a single mom, she never understood why her life was so difficult. She turned away from anything spiritual, believing she could never turn her life around. She later returned to it after having a vision. She's been immersing herself in anything spiritual or metaphysical, trying to help others that feel hopeless to find their way as well. She can help you turn your life around too!

Success Starts With Loving Yourself

By Renee Dean

It took me such a long, long time to stand in front of a mirror and look up and down and say I love you, because the truth is, I didn't. I couldn't. Love in my eyes was nothing, absolutely nothing. I felt disgusting and that I deserved everything I received. I believed I was lucky to have anyone to love me. I was a total waste of space, so I chose to seek self-validation through others. Through how *they* saw me, how *they* loved me, and how *they* validated me. I was entirely vulnerable to their thoughts and actions. I became what they saw in me: ugly, fat, useless, pathetic. They were masters at controlling, because *they* had low self-esteem (which is almost always a trait in people that control); and I believed everything I heard because I also had no self-esteem. But I was pre-determined by another person who had been in a similar situation as me and I couldn't recognize it. Because like attracts like, you literally attract what you are and if that isn't a recipe for disaster, I don't know what is! But that was all I knew at the time. It was all I wanted to know, because the truth is that it is *extremely* painful to face who you really are. The easier option is always to stay numb and continue the monotony of what you've become comfortable doing. However, the problem with that is that it gets you nowhere and leaves you in the same place—miserable and alone.

At the lowest point in my life, sunken into the deepest depths of depression, completely defeated by yet another failed relationship, I was suicidal; I had hit rock bottom. I remember sitting alone on the floor of my shower after drinking myself to death—or at least trying to. I looked up and there was something I had heard about but never believed in; there was a light. A big bright ray of sunshine beaming down on me as if the skies had opened up solely for me. I then heard a voice demand, "get up." And so I did, I walked to my living room as guided and the law of attraction was being talked about on television. I couldn't believe that something so easy could change your life with just 3 steps:

1. Ask

2. Receive

3. Believe

Needless to say, I fell into the law of attraction. I was in shock and awe and utter amazement. I felt something I hadn't felt, maybe ever—I felt passion. I quickly immersed myself as deeply as possible and sought out any author who wrote or spoke on the subject. I was willing to change my life; I was ready to change my life. The next day started with me standing in front of the mirror trying to see the person that was *behind* the person that was staring back at me, behind the person I knew. I had to learn to love myself. I had to stop this vicious, self-destructive cycle of allowing others to validate me. I got very real with myself and I had to think, how did I get here?

I was raised in a family with split beliefs. My mother, raised on a strict farm in North Dakota, was very devout to Western religion. My father, the Californian hippie, was very metaphysical. So, my parents made an arrangement when my brother and I were very little not to ever bring up the metaphysical part of their beliefs. My mother felt it was very important to raise devout church-going children, so my father agreed. However, my father would silently hand me books as a child or say certain phrases to me that would make me question these things I was being taught. To be honest, I thought he was crazy. I didn't understand a lot of the things he believed in and spent his life working on. Growing up, I acted out. I was always in and out of trouble. I've had failed marriages, abusive relationships, and DUIs. Alcohol was always my drug of choice because I wanted to be numb. I wanted to block out what I was feeling or not feeling. And I felt confident that I didn't deserve any better from myself than what I was giving.

The Change[11]

I was always attracted to motivational speakers and people with great lives. Growing up with so many challenges in my life, I never thought I was worthy of those thing. I thought these people deserved this because they were handed this life, they were born lucky or with silver spoons attached to their lips. Boy, was I wrong. As I dove into my studies, I was amazed to find that most of these inspirations to me were just like me. They had troubled childhoods, addictions, failed marriages, etc. Out of the rubble of these mistakes, they were able to grow, learn, and expand and teach others.

When I hit rock bottom, the first person I knew to call was my father. The first sentence out of my mouth was, "Dad, I'm ready." Followed abruptly by "Teach me everything you know. Why am I here? What's our purpose? What's my purpose?" I wanted to know how I could give back and teach what I know—which is pain and suffering. I wanted to get through it and teach others to get through it. I wanted to teach others to heal from their *own* pain and suffering. I wanted to be a compass for those who feel that they can't go any lower. I wanted to help them. And so I learned that it all starts with loving yourself. Nothing will unfold until you love yourself. The depths of the places you can go and the things you can achieve will never be unlocked to you until you believe, truly believe, that you are worthy of them. And the only reason any of us are here is simple—We are here to serve, and to give back. But it has to start with loving ourselves.

What are you worth? If you truly believe you come from greatness from whatever you choose to call the other side, God, The Universe, etc., if you can believe that you were created from the same likeness, you can believe that you were put here on purpose. There is a reason for your existence. And you can create great things. You are not here simply to clock in and clock out every day of your life. I promise you that. Regardless of your past or your mistakes, every day is a new day. And you should be grateful for those experiences because that darkness is what has brought you out here into the light. They have brought you here to change. And you're ready. That's why you bought this book—*The Change*. That's why you've attended this seminar—to change. If you take a $100 bill and crumple it up and step on it and deface it, it's still worth $100 when you open it. No matter what you've been through, your worth is the same. And you *have* to believe that in order to change your life. We are conditioned into thinking that we cannot escape ourselves; but you do not have to be imprisoned by your past. Only when you truly believe this can you drop the shackles of your former experiences and began to heal and really change.

How you are in your life right now, your current pattern of behaviors, are simply learned behaviors. Throughout your childhood, (good or bad) you learned what worked for you and have carried those learned behaviors with you all of your life. Undoing multiple years of behavior takes time and diligence—it's a process. But it is worth it. And I know you can do it, because I have.

Get real with yourself

You have to become raw and real with yourself in order to ever make any changes. Every day you lie to yourself, you push yourself further away from happiness and your best life. The mirror exercise works wonders for this. Get completely naked and stand in front of your mirror. Then look at yourself, I mean *really* look at yourself. Look up and down, analyze every part from your nose hairs to your toe nails. Then stare into your eyes uninterrupted and see behind your eyes. Know that this person is void of ego and can do and accomplish anything they put their mind to. Know that this person's opinion in the only one that truly matters. Don't take anything personal that another person says because we're all coming from different lives and what they've experienced in their life molds their opinions, **it has nothing to do with you.**

You attract what you are

Be VERY cautious with your thoughts. If you believe you're unworthy of happiness or success, what do you think you'll attract? If you believe you are wonderful and humble and worthy of life's gifts, what do you think you'll attract? And this applies to every single aspect of your life: relationships, career, family, etc. Once you truly believe you're better, you accept better.

Do not let go of the past

Over and over I read, "Let go of the past," but you mustn't. You must use the past as a learning tool. However, it is imperative that you let go of your *guilt* of the past. The Past was there for a very specific reason—it shaped who you are today. Everything done is very calculated by the other side. No one doing is without purpose. Yes, we have free will to stay on or get off your path. In order to not repeat what you've done, you must use your tools to make you stronger and push you forward.

The only moment that matters is right now

There is no future in your past. Thinking about the future brings worry and stress and thinking about the past brings guilt and shame. It is imperative that you stay in the present moment and *live* there. Every decision you make effects the present moment. Trust in your gut and your heart; they are the most important tools we have. Make confident decisions through *them* without fear of repercussion. There's a reason these tools were given to you. Let them guide you.

Be specific about what you want

And I mean really specific. Keep the specificity in your mind—do not let it wander and waver. Make a vison board. This is simply a cork board, or a poster board that you cut out, and paste to it the things you want or changes you would like to make in your life. Such as a car, a dream home, a career, a skinny person…whatever. Hang it in a place where you see it every day, and you see it often and when you look at it, close your eyes and believe. Believe that it's yours. Believe it's real. Believe it's all happening for you. And do not let anyone deter you from this. Not even YOURSELF. Every time you think a thought, it goes out into the universe and gets created. For this reason, be very careful what you think of yourself, what you think of your purpose, and what you think of your plans. You would never allow someone to talk negatively about you or your family or your life, so why would it be ok for you to do it to yourself? Cut any negative people in your life immediately. Find the scissors and start cutting. I know it can be hard sometimes, but it is so important. You can love them still, just from afar. Treat yourself like you belong to someone you love. Eventually, you will transform into someone you **do** love.

Take the Leap

Let go and jump off that cliff. If it's for something you are passionate about, you *will* fly. There are only two emotions that actually exist in this world—fear and love. Fear is the only thing that will drive you away from your goals, your happiness, your purpose, and the life you are *meant* to live. You have to retrain yourself to recognize and choose love. Choose love every time. It rules the entire universe—both sides. It's very scary to jump. It is terrifying, at first, to leave your current life behind for the one you deserve; to quit your job to move forward with what you want to do with your life. Remember, if it's what is in your gut and your heart, you will have the other side guiding you. You will have your purpose leading you to success. Never chase money. Remember that you're here to serve and the money will come. Remember that what you're doing now—whether it's clocking in and out of a job, marriage, or life you can't stand—**It isn't working**. So why not try something different? Believe in yourself, believe in your purpose, and take the Leap.

Take Action

Once you finally realize how important you are to this planet, how much we need you, and that you have a true purpose, you must take action. Take action on your dreams and goals that you've already been specific about. A goal list is absolutely imperative to accomplishing your goals. Make a goal list every single night with everything you want to accomplish the next day. What you don't get done, cross off and put on the top of the next day's list. Immerse yourself in information—read books, take seminars, scour the internet. This is the most important way to figure out where you're going and how to get there. It's going to be work, but because it is your purpose, it's going to be work you love to do. Whether your goal is to lose weight or gain financial success, remember to be as specific as possible. See it, feel it, believe it, then take action.

Once you can practice all 7 steps on a continual, daily basis, they will become a part of your life and you will see your life change in monumental ways that you never thought were possible. You will have the courage and the determination to take that leap and fulfill anything you have been waiting to do to your entire life. You will know your purpose. You will know why you are truly here and you will be truly happy….truly. You will finally know that happiness isn't something outside of you that you look for—it's inside of you. And always has been.

The last, but most important thing I want to share with you that ties all of these things together is **MEDITATION!** I absolutely cannot stress the importance of meditation. There are so many people intimidated by meditation, but it is so very simple. You can start with 10 minutes per day. I do 10 minutes in the morning and 10 minutes before bed. You simply close your eyes and try to dismiss any thoughts you have and sit in silence. It centers your mind and brings you back into alignment with source, God, the universe….whatever your name is for the power greater than us. And what this does is allows you to overcome any stress you have in your life with greater ease. You won't realize it at first, but you slowly begin to feel yourself not as quick to react or to get angry. This in turn brings more inner peace and happiness. It also allows you to connect with your spirit guide(s) (yes…we all have them) and receive any messages they may have for you. Not to mention the numerous health benefits of meditation such as lower blood pressure, reduced cancer risks, decreased cardiovascular disease risks, etc.

I have a beautiful ritual that I use in the morning that I learned along the way. I wake up and open my eyes and I say my "gratitudes." I list everything I am grateful for that day. Then when my feet hit the ground, each footstep is a thank you. So I literally walk and say "thank you, thank you, thank you," all the way to the bathroom. Then I say it brushing my teeth.

Then I look at myself in the mirror and I say an affirmation of some kind. "You are good enough" or "I am ready to receive abundance." I also use a dry erase marker to write affirmations on my mirror. I read them every day and I change them often. Remember that the law of attraction states that you attract what you are. Daily affirmations send clear messages into the universe of exactly that.

Don't get overwhelmed with all of these changes. These are all things that are very easy to incorporate into your life. The best part is you will quickly start to see changes. You will feel better…happier through the day. And when you are happy, the people you are around get happy and you attract happy people. Pretty soon, you will be a magnet attracting all of the things you want and desire. Please understand, you will still go through hard times. Know that these are necessary in life for growth. There is no such thing as a problem without a gift in its hands. But, the way you look at it, the way you understand it, and most importantly, the way you **REACT** to it will be different. And you get over it and you move on to the next happy thought because you love yourself so much.

I said it earlier and I will say it again: What you are doing is not working. How about trying something else? What would you have to lose? You might fail and go back to your old life. You are doing that already. So take the leap!

***

reneedeanlifesuccesscoach.com

EMAIL:renee@reneedeanlifesuccesscoach.com

702 - 900 - 4760

Facebook: Renee Dean

Twitter : Renee_Dean

Crystal Areal

Having coached and mentored many companies, teams, and individuals for almost two decades, Ms. Areal has transformed executives, entrepreneurs, and housewives.

Crystal has taken her coaching skills and combined them with trainings on transformation, productivity, and communication. She has taught courses and led workshops for sales teams, Information Technology companies, large corporations, and start-up companies. Crystal's charisma, knowledge, effectiveness, and passion provide profound transformational results.

Ms. Areal's passions include writing, reading, roller derby, Boston terriers, and Chihuahuas. She is currently producing several video series on YouTube including a cooking show with her son that aims to teach children (and parents) how to cook.

"Crystal brought her expertise as a Coach and her talent for herding cats to our company and created an environment where development is being tracked and the geeks working with her are enjoying their subjugation. She helped us to track our progress and facilitated the emergence of self-governing teams who feel empowered to strive continually towards improvement. It's not an easy task, but she made it look easy, and the flow into the changing processes was smooth and felt natural. We needed someone like her, and I'm very glad we had her here."

K. WOLFE

The Seven Day Habit

By Crystal Areal

Have you ever wondered why some people just seem to have it all? They drive great cars, live in amazing houses and always look picture perfect. They walk around with a spring in their step and nothing seems to faze them. They are free from debt, have phenomenal relationships, and maybe even have kids that are more polite than your grandparents. Who waved their magic wand and granted these people the perfect lives?

They did. That's right, they waved their own wand, and I'm going to teach you how to do the exact same thing. Everything you are, everything you want to become, and everything you will be is all up to you. You have the power to wave the magic wand and give yourself your ideal life.

People like I've described above usually have at least one thing in common: they have *success* habits. According to science (and maybe a little bit of magic), 95 percent of everything that humans do, think, and feel is a direct result of their habits. More importantly, 95 percent of everything we achieve in life is due to our habits. Think about that for a minute. Let it sink in.

What are your habits manifesting in your life right now? Are you often sick? Is your house always a mess? Do you have a business that is just…meh? I'll bet that if you stop and think about it, you can trace all of these things back to your habits, or lack thereof.

Let's take, for example, someone who has a constantly messy house. I'm going to venture a guess that they don't have a habit of putting things away immediately after use. They probably also don't have a habit of cleaning up as they cook dinner. They may even just let their mail pile up on the front table and overflow into the hallway because they don't have a habit of opening things immediately, paying the bill, filing it, or recycling it. I could go on and on, but I'm sure you get my point.

Insights into Self-Empowerment

This chapter is an introduction to my book and YouTube series, *The 7 Day Habit*. The book, video series, and accompanying downloadable materials will help you learn how to use the magic wand you already have. You will to learn how to identify what habits you need (and want) to adopt, and how to do it quickly and effectively.

Today, I want to give you something you can use immediately, and if you grab the book or watch the series later, that's great. If not, that's ok, too! I want you to learn how to identify your habit needs and wants and create an action plan around them. I want you to learn to wield your own magic wand. Let's get started!

First, I want to dispel the myth that a habit takes twenty-one days to create. This is simply not true. I go into full detail on this in my book, but the short version of the story is this: Over half a decade ago, a plastic surgeon noticed a trend among his patients. They would typically take around 21 days to get used to their new faces, or in the case of amputees, to stop feeling phantom limb symptoms. This doctor also noticed that he himself took around 21 days on average to begin doing something consistently once he had set out to achieve a new goal. He published a quote in what became a top selling book and that quote was turned into a game of "telephone" by some prominent self-help gurus who eventually shortened his quote to "It takes 21 days to form a habit." That misstated quote has since spread like wildfire and is often stated as a statistical fact.

The truth of the matter is, a scientific study was completed that indicates it actually takes an average of sixty-six days to create a habit, but the range is anywhere from eight days to eight months, with some habits taking far less time, and some taking far more time to form.

So why are you sitting here reading about The 7 Day Habit if a habit takes an average of sixty-six days to form? Because I am of the firm belief that anyone can do anything for seven days, and what's important is that you begin the process! If you follow my program, you will learn the process for identifying habits, why you need them, and what it takes to get them ingrained in your psyche. By following The 7 Day Habit process, you will be well on your way to forming a solid habit. Not only that, but seven days is long enough for you to identify if you even want to keep the habit in your life or not. Not all habits you identify are ones you'll want to keep!

Let's start by identifying a habit you want to bring into your life. If you're anything like I used to be, you often tell yourself you're going to start doing something, and you may even start it, repeating the new thing a few times before you give up. Why do we do this? I know for me personally, it's because I didn't really think the new thing through. I didn't identify my "why." I'll give you an example.

I wanted to start running every day. I'm not a runner. Heck, I'm not even a walker! But I came across this program called C25K (Couch to 5k) and it seemed like something I could do. They had a great sales pitch that appealed to my couch potato people. I could do this! So I told myself that starting tomorrow, I was going to start running every single day. Can you guess how long this lasted? Exactly one day. At first, I just hung my head in shame and decided it was just me giving up on yet another goal. I became depressed that I had failed. Looking back on it now, I realize it's because I wasn't prepared to bring that particular habit into my life. I hadn't thought it through at all.

I'm getting ready to start this particular program again, but this time I'm doing it the right way. I will succeed, because I'm preparing my brain for receiving this new habit. I'm using The 7 Day Habit process. Let's go into what that looks like.

THE 7 DAY HABIT PROCESS

Step 1: Identify your need
Step 2: Identify the benefits of implementing a new habit
Step 3: Identify the habit(s) that will fill your need
Step 4: Choose one habit to focus on for the next 7 days and detail it out.
Step 5: Implement your habit for 7 days
Step 6: Evaluate how it went

Step 7: Choose whether to keep, modify, or chuck your habit
Repeat the process once per new habit!

To identify a habit you want to bring into your life, you must first identify a need. Then you can go through the 7 Day Habit process. I'll use the running example above, and we'll walk through the exercise together. Note that when identifying a need, it may very well have several habits associated with it. It's not always a one to one need to habit ratio.

Step 1: Identify your NEED (or want) - I need to start exercising. I have lived a very sedentary life and my immune system hasn't been the greatest. I've recently lost quite a bit of weight, but haven't done the exercise needed to tone up and keep my muscles in decent shape. My strength is probably not what it should be for a woman of my age, and I'd like to get my endurance up there, too, so I can go hiking with my kids and not get winded on my roller derby skates after five minutes.

Step 2: Identify the BENEFITS - Once I start exercising, I will feel better physically, mentally, and emotionally. I will tone up my weak muscles. I will increase my strength and endurance. I will be able to roller skate for longer periods of time without getting winded. I will be able to go to Silver Falls with my family and not dread a short hike that other people can do with their eyes closed. I will set a good example for my kids by moving my body daily. I will feel and look more attractive and this will help me feel more confident around my spouse. I will inspire others who may be having a hard time starting new healthy habits.

Step 3: Identify NEW HABIT(S) - C25K program; Daily Yoga

Step 4: Choose this week's FOCUS HABIT - C25K
HABIT DETAILS: The C25K Program is a downloadable app on iOS or Android devices. All I have to do is pick a time every day and start the app. It will lead me through everything step by step. It's an 8-week program, and by the end, I should be able to run a 5k marathon without stopping.

Step 5: BEGIN!

HABIT START DATE: 6/22/16
DAY 1 ___
DAY 2 ___
DAY 3 ___
DAY 4 ___
DAY 5 ___
DAY 6 ___
DAY 7 ___

Step 6: 7 DAY EVALUATION - At this point, you will look back over the past seven days (which hopefully all have checkmarks by them) and evaluate this new habit you've chosen to focus on. You will write in your 7 Day Habit Notebook (where you'll be keeping all of the downloadable worksheets and printables available from my website) a detailed account of how this past week has made you feel. This evaluation exercise is an important part of The 7 Day Habit process. Don't skip it!

Step 7: KEEP IT, MODIFY IT, OR CHUCK IT - Is this a habit that you feel is still beneficial? It's ok to say no! Not all habits are ones we need or want to keep. On the other hand, if you feel amazing and you're seeing those benefits you detailed above, you'll want to keep this habit in your arsenal and you'll move it to the *keep* section of your notebook.

That's it! See how simple this process is? You can take these seven steps and repeat them over and over again until you have your very own set of success habits, which we'll call your Magic Wand. It doesn't matter that you've only done your new habit for seven days at this point. It is now solidly ingrained in your mind because you've detailed out why you're doing it and what the benefits are. You didn't start this habit all willy nilly just because it sounded like the thing to do. You followed the process and waved your magic wand.

In *The 7 Day Habit* book and on the YouTube series, you'll find hundreds of habits already detailed out for you, including benefits and detailed instructions on carrying the habits out. I've already done part of the work for you, but you'll need to do the hard work of choosing which habits meet your particular needs and get you closer to your individual goals. You'll need to go through the process, try the habits out, and choose which ones to keep, modify, or chuck. Soon you'll have your Success Habits notebook in order and you'll watch your life go from chaos and disorganization to calm, order, and abundance!

Here is a small sampling of ideas to get you started. You'll find all of these habits fully detailed out, along with printable downloads to follow along with at The7DayHabit.com.

Mind Habits

Affirmations
Gratitude
Getting Creative
One Thing at a Time
Write
Learn a Language
Get Social
Stay Positive
Learn something new
Meditation
Unplug
Say no
Spend time in nature
Play with a pet
Spend time in the sun
Watch less TV
Have a morning routine
Goal setting
Procrastination
Write a thank you note
Dream board
Pray
Do something out of your comfort zone
Pay attention to promptings

Body Habits

Vitamins
Sleep
Exercise
Cut out sugar
Eat only real foods
Hydrate
Stop drinking soda
Cook healthy dinners
Cook meals in advance
Add veggies to each meal
Cut out gluten
Add probiotics
Add omega 3s
Healthy breakfast
Eat until 80% full
Keep a food journal
Try yoga
Decrease toxic chemicals
Brush/floss twice daily
Wash face twice daily
Eat mindfully

Financial Habits

Spend less
Track every penny
Don't buy on impulse
Open bills immediately
Don't use credit cards
Save on groceries
Faithfully follow budget
Save daily
Round up every purchase
Learn how to invest
Add prosperity affirmations
Donate

Household Habits

Plan meals in advance
Plan your next day's outfit
Declutter daily
Minimize
Deep clean something
Follow cleaning routine
Make your bed
Check your guest view
Go through your closet
Go through your food
Go through your cabinets

Habits for Kids

Brush/floss teeth
Pick up room
Set out school clothes
Review homework w/mom
Daily chores
Daily affirmations
Ask "what can I do for you today"
Write a thank you note
Learn to cook
Learn a language
Show appreciation
Dream board
Pray
Pick a toy to donate

Relationship Habits

Actively socialize with friends
Laugh and smile
Be more giving
Be intimate more often
Forgive
Call someone you love
Write a letter
Love notes

Ask "what can I do for you today?"
Self-review
Play a family game

Work/Business Habits

IPAs every day (Income Producing Activities)
Ask "what can I do for you today?"
Add to your list
Review your goals
Daily affirmations
Goal setting
Self-performance review
Follow up
Send a thank you card
Review your action plan
Maintain good records
Blog daily
Research daily
3-Item To-Do-List
Delegate
Talk about what you do

***

To contact Crystal:

CrystalAreal.com
The7DayHabit.com
YouTube.com/CrystalAreal
SOCIAL MEDIA:
Facebook.com/workwithcrystal
Twitter @crystalareal
Instagram @crystalareal
Pinterest @crystalareal
Snapchat @crystalareal

Bob J. Heron

Bob J Heron takes an interest in people and their challenging situation to show them the way to their dreams and goals. Bob had been a successful electrician, job steward, entrepreneur, and author. He is on a change of life and career journey to become a life and self-discovery coach. Bob started his new journey in 2015 after he was laid off from his job. That was the spark that started his discovery and opened the doorway to his new life and career. He is learning to help others while discovering himself. Bob is aligning himself with his passion and enjoying the excitement of the experience. He wants to focus on small seminars and open up a diabetic help group that helps those newly diagnosed and people who are getting lost with the medical rhetoric like he was. Bob lives in Thorsby, Alberta, Canada.

The Power of Self-Influence
By Bob J. Heron

We often do not realize how others influence our decisions. As a child, this can be a great thing, or not so great! As I traveled through my life journey, I realized the only true *"influence"* I need to listen to is myself. It's really easy to allow past experiences, whether from childhood, friends, relationships, parents, co-workers, and even television to affect us without realizing what's happening. We can get off course at times, and then we think, "How did I get here"!

When I was a really young child—we're talking four years old—I had instincts and intuition about life that made me different. School for me was a time of avoiding bullies or letting the bullies know who was boss—ME! Some say *"normal boy stuff"*—rock fights, name calling, being a loner. I think back to the beginning of school; four of my friends and I gathered at the end of my driveway. It was late summer and preparations for the new school buzzed around me. My friends were excited about going to school and it just didn't thrill me. I thought that going to school then going to work after didn't look like much fun. I watched my dad live this process, day in and day out. The provider, working long hours to provide these back to school items, which I deemed unnecessary. The thought of beginning this training was depressing. I didn't understand why, it just was.

All through elementary school, I never fit in. *The lone wolf*, I didn't want to join in on what in my mind was the boring conversations or rhetoric. Instead, I was always interested in music and loved drumming. This became my anger outlet and passion. My self-imposed influence to deal with the outside world I didn't understand. Then in high school, I went through scary gangs coming at me, incidents which actually toughened me up and gave me the courage to know when something wrong, something had to be done to stop it.

I then became a bouncer for school dances and concerts. I first discovered I had the knack of cooling people down, influencing them with my words before things got out of hand. I learned that it was not the size of the person who wins the fight but the fight in the person: *meaning desire and strength to never give up. With persistence through life, I have both battled following the crowd and yet trying to break free. As I had my own children, these battles were no longer about me. My mind took away this identity and made me a father.*

I have two amazing boys and I am Grandpa of a beautiful little girl that has stolen my heart. It took this little angel for me to realize that the process I'm sharing with you now was the only way to understand that my love for my family was very important. The challenge was figuring out what I needed to learn, change, and remain committed to in order to spend the time I so desired to be present in the life of my boys and my grand-daughter.

I have always had the *"entrepreneur"* spirit. I always have been taught to "Work hard, get those benefits, take care of the family," leaving me with a desire for more of EVERYTHING! More time, more love, more experiences with my family, more money, great relationships, and soon enough I would receive more fear…something I didn't bargain for.

On August 12, 2015, I got the call, the *"pink slip,"* the laid off notice! I don't know if deep down it truly was really *"fear."* The fear I felt was geared more towards the income aspects because so much of me was saying, *"I am glad I no longer have to fill my days with these people I'm surrounded by."* The complaining from "all about ME" people, yet they never did anything about any of their complaints.

It was in this moment that I realized my mixed emotions could be a good thing. What if they led me to discover something truly great? I was going to take this opportunity and do what I wanted. I knew I had a passion in me that was left untapped, I just didn't know how to get to it. What was the vehicle and where would it come from?

The Change[11]

What I was certain of was that working for someone else was something I never desired. The hours I worked for the vision of others, instead of my own, felt like I was just logging hours! The divorces, the many obstacles that led me to this very moment, all were just forms of logging hours. Becoming fed up with the double standards in the construction industry and the world, I again found myself influenced by a job. Why was I focused on working for someone else and their dream? I kept silently telling myself there had to be a better way. What were my dreams, my passions?

I sorted through many "careers." I always wanted my own business. Possibly a counselor type position, because really I wanted to help other people. I went down the list of possibly doing something with animals, then I realized, no I just love my own! I continued down the list of possibilities…inventing, building, something I could wrap my heart and mind around. Still I was always running this and that by my boys or others in my life and everyone had an opinion, an influence, which I took to heart. It brought me to such confusion that I wasn't sure where I was going. If you've worked in the corporate world, have you ever felt stuck and unrecognized for all you were doing?

Oddly, I tabled the entire idea of STARTING OVER. It was a lot of work so I left it—it took too much to think about. Though I was unaware at the time, I just felt it was exhausting to continue going over these issues and ideas. With absolutely no resolve in sight, I decided to let it go. Sometimes when you leave things alone, they fix themselves. When you stop overthinking these things and remove our egos is when the solutions begin to become clear.

Over several months, I spent (or shall I say ignored) my days with what I thought was enjoying life. I spent my days being, well, lazy! I had coffee, took naps, and I did whatever, whenever, and however. I had little regard for LIVING as I was just passing time. Maybe you have done the same. A sense of denial, no one is looking, therefore I do as I please. I have no one to check in with, no places to be, and honestly it just felt good for a change. As I rediscovered I was really just checked out and wanted to see what life would be like if... I had no place to be any given time. If I didn't have to listen to people and their opinions, I was free.

There it was, in my head—FREE!! Was I free? What is free? I'm not financially solid, I'm laid off! I'm acting as though I have found my purposes, but what does that mean, "my purpose"? How do I find it? Where do I go with this newfound "FREE"? I was not free at all, in fact. I had free time because I was doing nothing except waiting.

These are great questions, I thought. This is what I need to ask myself—"What is free"? I have been influenced by others, doing what is expected. Even bullied by people in my life and wondering how I got here from there, and how do I get back, to me! Every moment felt like I turned new corners. I had stopped replaying the reel of what was expected and started a new movie in my head of what I wanted. I had no idea what I was embarking on and I knew I had to keep searching. Find the new "actors" in my new movie. The director, producer, and the star—me. Figure out my plot for my life, with input only from myself. I recall literally asking the Universe, ***"What is my purpose"?***

As past comments and ideas came into my head, I considered whether these were mentors talking to me. Can they influence me to listen to what they have to say and take action? Or was this more self-chatter? What was I supposed to allow to have an effect on me? The true mentors made me feel, not just think. I knew when I felt the happiest, being fulfilled, loving myself, was when I was helping others to do this very same thing—*INFLUENCE YOURSELF* and take action for yourself.

It was the experts in my head telling me I already knew these answers. Already feeling a sense of relief, which inspired me to call a friend. It had been several months since we had talked and I reached out to her, kind of selfishly wanting to know if she could help me or had some ideas. I remember this so clearly because she didn't influence me, she gave me options!

I recall the conversation and as vulnerable as I was, I told her my story. That I felt like I had wasted the last 5 months of my life. It was hard to admit this, telling her I had spent my time in my recliner, and she shared with me exactly what I needed. She was in a business which had the programs I had been searching for. This was exciting and hopeful! I knew this could work for me. Like nothing before I dove into this program of self-awareness, of moving forward, self-observation, and letting go. As scary as this journey could be, it also felt so good to release all this "stuff." I jumped right on in. The water was warm and comforting, yet still full of energy and a new sense of hope and resolution washed over me.

As the days continued, I felt so alive and so aware, telling myself, "Yes, the only one that I can be ***influenced*** by is myself." It was up to me to take the material and apply it. It was up to me to be committed to the process and I was. I listened to the programs and I began to notice moments that had meaning. Then I noticed my attitude was changing and what others said really had no effect on me. Not to suggest I didn't care what people were saying, I do care about people and this was the difference, I just didn't have to absorb their energy. I had mentors and I listened, I took action in their teachings, I was on my way to be FREE of all the influences that held me back. I decided I would take this offering, and I would use it for myself and others. I knew if I felt the way I did, so would other people and there in that moment, I found the answers. I help myself and I then can help others.

I thought about being on an airplane: "If there should be an emergency and you're traveling with small children or those needing help, please put the oxygen mask on yourself first and then assist others." Putting the metaphoric oxygen mask on, I began to breathe. Relaxing and understanding I had not failed, I was removed from a place where I was afraid of staying forever and clocking in forever. It was allowing room for new ventures to show up in my life. Ventures with endless opportunity to change my path and help others do the same. We grow up watching the important people around us, submitting to these rules, because that is what they knew and I now would break that cycle, for me, my children, and many more to follow.

Connecting the dots now in my life, I saw how easily we could stay in our comfort patterns. I remember calling it a "rut." I looked up the word "rut" and read in the description the word "turn." So I looked up the word turn in the dictionary, and this was the moment I knew I had officially turned my life around: Turn is a noun; ***an opportunity or obligation to do something that becomes successively to each of a number of people.*** OKAY! I need to take my turn to help others with their opportunity to turn.

Whatever success and moving on means to each person was for them to decide, just as I decided this was my contribution—to share my turn of events. This is why so many suffer with low self-esteem, and don't have to. Why the negative mind chatter can take over, being told what is expected of you, instead of being authentic and respecting you. Now I can show people how to decide what is an influence verses a circumstance and show them how to turn their lives towards what really matters—your true self. I would help people come back to life, just like myself! The excitement of this journey was overwhelming in a way I've never recognized, even in myself. I noticed how paralyzed I had been. Not truly living and now, I had let all of this go and I could see freedom in color. I didn't have to talk myself out of doing anything or into anything. Now instead, I was fearless and telling others of my newfound excitement for life. When I came to a fork in the road (you know, where you don't actually see the signs but they read "past" to the left, "future" to the right), veering right, I continued this self-influential feeling, and if felt right, it felt full of purpose. It's happened to me more times than I realized and what was different this time was I recognized it, because I had learned to let go of influences that were no longer useful. It became simple and easy to move forward and not be bound by others' opinions of what I should be doing. Immediately, I was grateful for this experience. Mainly because I was awake and aware of my potential, which I'm not sure I had ever truly been.

The Change[11]

As I continued connecting the dots, I thought about the time I joined a business, separate from my "job," and I recalled the gentleman that introduced me to the business telling me, "You'll make director soon and be set!" *Set for what?* I now thought, and I let those words influence me… yes I will make director and be set! Now I looked back on this, and I realized I took this message literally. I almost made director and you know I had one more person to go to become director and I quit! It hit me like a ton of bricks, *"I QUIT AFTER I DID WHAT I WAS TOLD!"* This was a major revelation. Now I set my goals, and I will not quit at any level. After all, how can I help others if I quit? As I continued to learn more about my ability to influence myself, I started to dig a little further. As I worked on staying in the NOW and not falling back into the old patterns I was so used to, I could see how much faster it was for me to change from negative to positive. Testing myself to keep asking and exploring.

This process of moving forward, with the attitude of a winner, I began to meet people on the same path as myself. I met life coaches and people involved in personal development—it seemed as if they were everywhere. I'm sure they always had surrounded me; I just never took notice. It's kind of like when you have a desire for a certain car, or anything, but let's use a car in this analogy. When you are so focused on buying a certain car, you do not notice how many there are till you own one yourself. As I changed the way I saw myself and believed in my confidence to help others that may have learned logging hours was their only choice in life, I also began to meet people who answered only to themselves. Influencing themselves and when influencing others, it was purely in a positive direction only. There wasn't anyone judging, or spouting opinions of my decisions. Or maybe they were and I just didn't need their opinions any longer.

As I am so excited to share this with you and write this chapter, I share with you my lesson. There was no room for me to dwell in my laid off state, while pursuing another opportunity that made me feel alive and awake. No longer allowing distractions to interfere with my focus, which was a battle and here is a hint to organize your thoughts, such as I did. I sat down and wrote out all my daily activities and decided which ones were helping and which ones were not and to let go of those which were not for my greater goals in life. I thought I had gone through this a couple of times during my quest; really I had not learned how to commit to let go and be thankful for being offered what was to become my passion in life. *Helping others get out of their "rut" and take the "turn" into newfound purpose.*

Influences come from everywhere in life. Mom and Dad, Grandparents, family, friends, and neighbors. Doctors, Pharmacist, Teachers, and other vocational professions. We must learn to utilize influences which are for the best in ourselves. Those that are for our greater good and in our life path. Those that keep us on track and make sense, to each of us individually. It's a choice, not an influence, however contagious it may be. I spent a good portion of my life logging hours for others, and now I help others and assist them to log their own hours and follow their dreams.

We get as many chances as we want, if we are willing to start over and this is by no means done by chance.

***

To contact Bob:

1-587-784-9044

or by email.

info@bobheron.net

Marco Valerio Ricci

Marco Valerio Ricci is the creator of the D-K.a.l.t. Yourself Coaching model to help his clients to get out of the collective hypnosis that prevents them from living in a 3D, 4K, and full Dolby Surround life enjoying the journey of their lives every day.

Marco Valerio is an international renowned Licensed NLP Master Trainer with the Society of NLP, a Clinical Hypnosis Trainer for the Wessex College of Hypnosis and NLP in UK, a Hypnotist, and a Sport, Life, and Business Coach.

He fluently Trains and Coaches in English, French and, of course, Italian, both in person, through webinars and via Skype. His clients come from every walk of life, from multinational corporations such as Pfizer and MSD, to the Italian National Rugby Team, to International Skiers and Figure Skaters, to entrepreneurs and solopreneurs, up to people that want to work on their communication skills and abilities in creating their perfect relationship.

Since 2008, he has been part of the international team of assistants of Dr. Richard Bandler during his international trainings. He is the author of two books that will soon be translated in English, and of a series of CDs for self-hypnosis with 432z music.

Everything Is Perfect as It Is
How to create a plan and forget it to reach an extraordinary life

By Marco Valerio Ricci

It was a day in the middle of April 1996. I had just finished speaking to an audience of about 30 people and a couple of them came to me saying, "You know Lieutenant Ricci, whenever you speak you leave us something more."

And my internal thinking was "What can it be, since I'm talking about nuclear, chemical, and biological war?"

Little did I know at the time how those words were then predictive of a future that already was inside me. Not too long after those times, my life suddenly got in a stuck situation that, from the point of view of the knowledge I have now, was the "perfect" turning point from which I got in the exact path that has led me where I am now, twenty years later.

When I left the army, a series of setbacks led to question myself, my worthiness, and the deep meaning of life. I felt hopeless.

But my past had also taught me that there must have been something for me, in this life. It couldn't be over. And so, my quest started.

I started defying my limits, looking for something (I didn't know what it was), but I knew for sure that it was somewhere. I was only missing the where then, which is inside me. I started following seminars and studying personal growth, self-help and communication, NLP and coaching and amazingly something started to change...magically.

Yes, you know, when "The Change" arrives, it seems so easy that it feels as if magic is happening. Was it possible that that young guy, who used to feel unworthy, all of a sudden was feeling successful and the results in his life were showing?

Is it possible that the change is so easy and seemingly effortless? The answer was, and still is, yes...and no. Further in this chapter, I will go deeper in this affirmation, but before explaining it, you need to have some more elements in this story, to get to use the teachings that you can get from it, from me and from the process it helped me create.

My results were so astonishingly good in every area of my life that I wanted to learn more. I was feeling I could become a "superhero"...

Month by month, I started getting more and more involved in the fields of NLP and Coaching, which have become my main field for influencing in changing people's lives for slightly less than two decades now.

As I recall those days in my memory, I also recall that person that was listening to the words of his soldiers. When this story started, I was someone who felt public speaking was one of the main threats to his own security, and that he wasn't worth what he had been given by life. Mostly I was confused about my future, my present, and whatever I was living. At the time, I didn't even have a girlfriend and my whole life seemed to center around doing something in the army instead of being someone for myself.

From that point, the research I started for myself has led me to connect the dots of my life into something that, looking from the stand point of the future, is the only thing that could've been happening to my life, becoming who I am now...and being proud of myself. How could that have been possible for a guy that was aware he had only hopes, but, I thought, he had no chances? The answer is in the exact same model of Coaching I have developed ever since.

With that in mind, I approach writing about what I think is the most important thing for someone who wants to change his life: having a plan and forgetting it!

If, for any reason, the question you have in mind is "What's the purpose of having a plan, if I have to forget about it?", well, I understand your curiosity. Keep reading till the end and you'll get complete satisfaction.

But first of all, think about how many times we try and plan things perfectly and try to stick to the plan, but things don't work the way we have planned! What if you would discover that the right path was what you got instead of what you wanted?

I must admit that the same thing happened to me many times in my life. And it also happened about ten years ago when I set out to discover what was the thing that made the difference between two groups of people that I noticed came out of coaching processes. The first group was the people that were able to reach and fulfill their goals through Coaching and then had to go back to a coach when they had a situation or a new goal to reach, even of the same level of the previous one. The second group were those people that were able to generalize the learnings from the process of Coaching. That is, once they had reached their goals, they would become able to reach whatever goal at that specific level of difficulty or challenge, not having to ask for the support of a Coach other than for a new and completely different level of goals.

What I have discovered in my quest is astonishing and, especially if you are aware of the teachings from different ancient cultures, it seems as if it would come out from the mixing of that knowledge. I think in every age of humankind, there are ways of applying old learnings that bring you to a breakthrough to new understandings. The roots of this something new can easily be spotted in history, but that's not everything that is in there. Saying that's only the same old story that repeats itself is like thinking that the Earth rotates around the Sun in an elliptical path and thinking that's the reality of things… that would be considering a context from a too small point of view! Since the Sun and the Solar System are spinning around the center of the Milky Way, the Earth is more likely moving in some kind of spiral around the Sun, and we could even consider getting to bigger contexts…if we would like or need. With that said, here I am stating the very first and most important consideration of all:

"Everything is PERFECT exactly as it is." And I know from experience how this makes so many people feel and what so many think: "But I don't like it at all!" "How can this be perfect if I feel stuck in this situation?" "I want to change, I don't want some kind of new age stuff that tells me to let it go" and so many similar protests. In other words, people want to get rid of their problems, and I agree, none deliberately wants to have problems, obstacles, or setbacks!

Then again, I always say that when you find obstacles that prevent you from getting to your goals—you could call them problem if you would—they are there only to tell you at which level you are at that moment, nothing else. Thanks to this, the D-K.a.l.t. Yourself Model helps you to go through the change in a way that is not pure "will power"; it is by accepting what it is and learning how to flow, not against the current, but by using the power of the stream to push and drive you exactly where you want to go and thrive while you are doing it. How does it work and what does this acronym stands for?

Well, the sound D-K.a.l.t. Yourself is very similar to de-cult yourself—that is "take away" yourself from the cults you are in. What are these "cults"? They are what I call collective hypnosis, ideas, beliefs, and behaviors that are commonly proposed and accepted by the culture you live in for the pure sake of surviving in that culture. What I have discovered is that to reach that change that you want and the sensation of freedom, you need to undergo a five step process that takes you from learning to behave and act in order to be able to get your results to being the person that lives in the state in which those results are normal. Let's now get deeper in the model and let's start going through this process one step at the time.

D - Discover Yourself

It might seem obvious to most people who are passionate about self-improvement or Coaching, but still it is not that clear for the majority of people, even for many of the so-called professionals of change. Most of the people out there are not aware of themselves, of what they do, and how they do it. The first three questions I always ask during seminars or Coaching sessions are: "What do you want?"; "What are you doing?"; and "How do you get to do what you are doing?"

They are powerful questions to help you to start getting some insights about yourself. Oftentimes even the first, simple question, "What do you want?" becomes important. So many people are focusing on what causes pain or problems or constitutes an obstacle that they forget to clarify for themselves what the outcome is that they really want to reach. Nothing bad nor particularly new about this. Except for the fact that that's the main reason for which those people just don't get the life they want! Because they just don't know that the first step to get something is to determine all those elements that will help you to recognize the path to follow to reach your dreams. And that knowing them will activate your entire mind and body system toward the identification of the opportunities that will help you get to the results you want.

Start asking these three question, both for important and common things, and listen to your body…your discoveries will lead you to get ready for the next step.

K - Know yourself

Too many people underestimate the difference between discovering and knowing. They ask, "But if I have discovered, then I now know, right?" Well, let's say that you need to discover, in the sense of unveil yourself to yourself, to get to know something, but knowing yourself means that you have developed a deep understanding of how your living system works and you are becoming aware of which changes work for you, how you respond to them. You also need to become able to chose which are the best strategies that you can adopt to get where you want to go. That said, the process to get you there is not that complicated, complex maybe, but easy to learn and manage.

Let's say you have the habit of having difficulties in making the right choice for you and in the Discover Yourself part you have become aware of the fact that every time you attempt to make a new one a memory from a bad choice in the past comes to your mind. Maybe it's an image of the unwanted consequences of your choice accompanied by an authoritarian voice that says "You're good for nothing, not even this time!" Now what can you do? Well, from NLP we know that if you change the qualities of your internal representation (for NLP experts, we call them submodalities), you are able to change the feelings and the chemistry of your system while thinking of that past event. Once you have learnt that, you can unlearn the "learned helplessness" about choosing.

First of all, take note of the following questions:

Are you inside the image or do you see it dissociated?

Is the memory black or white or in full color?

What's the size of the image?

Where do you see it? In front of you, on the sides, somewhere else…

If it is dissociated from you, how distant is the image?

Is it a still picture, a series of pictures, or a movie?

Is it dark or brilliant?

What about the voice? Does it come from a particular place?

What's the volume of it?

What's the tempo and the speed?

Once you have identified all these characteristics, just play with them, one at the time, and notice which changes make the feeling better and which make it feel even worse. And then just keep only the changes that make you feel better or definitely good…your brain, that's smarter than you might think, will keep those changes for good. If not, you can just do it again!

A. - Accept Yourself

Acceptance is the turning key that I found for the whole process of freeing yourself from public hypnosis, that are whatever we accept in order to be prevented from getting where we want. Once you have got this one, your road to change starts to go downhill. Acceptance is the way we free ourself from any emotional connection with whatever has happened in our past or will happen in the future. What acceptance is not: it is not resignation, nor giving up.

Acceptance is the means to let go of what I call your "residual image" of yourself. That is that sort of ghost of your old self that is created by all those presuppositions in your behaviors and habits that come from your past that you still show and tolerate whenever you are not consciously thinking about your actions and what you are doing in your life. Think about the former smoker that still is used to putting his hand in his pocket and then just remembers that he doesn't smoke anymore. Well that person still has the residual image of a smoker and sooner or later, in a moment of stress, his unconscious behavior will make it simple for him to go back to smoke.

How do you work on acceptance? Well, there are several paths and the one that I prefer is energetically, which is a means that's not easily explicable through the pages of a book. But I teach it during some specific trainings.

There are also some linguistic techniques that will work wonderfully for you. The very first and probably the most important one is changing to the past tense every reference, behavior, and thought about what you were before the change you made. To make it stronger, write on a piece of paper any of the behaviors or actions or thoughts that are still popping up in your mind that are linked to the past and once a week, make a fire of them while pronouncing the mantra "It's all gone now, I'm now free." When you stop fighting against something, you stop giving power to that something. When you stop complaining about something, you let your energy go in another direction and stop nurturing the "thing" from your past.

L - Love Yourself

The people who really were able to generalize their change do another thing that differentiates them from the others. They don't look outside for what they need. They give it to themselves. That's what I call Love Yourself. If you are in love with someone, you don't do it so that you will recieve back love by giving love to that person. When you give yourself what you need first, you will free yourself from emotional dependance upon others. Here you can use some more positive talk to yourself, combined with the energetic switch. Just hit the outer side of your right fist against your palm and then change hands while doing the same and saying "I love and accept myself with my freedom. I love and accept myself also without my freedom."

Notice the different feelings. You are now ready to:

T - Trance-Form Yourself

Have you ever noticed how hard it is to unlearn something you do well, with purpose? The fact is that when we make The Change in our lives, and learning means changing, we not only do things differently, we are different. Especially, our inner state has changed. That is, we are in the correct trance state to perform that change. We have reached the "identity" of the person that has changed, definitely and forever. To do so use meditation and self-hypnosis to associate you to the correct brainwave frequency that makes you free of being yourself.

Why is it important to live differently? Going around this world, I noticed how most people live: unaware, unconscious of themselves, depressed, sad, angry, and fearful. We live in a world that is at a turning point. We will either be free human beings or we will become the new slaves. Let's be honest, in human history, Homo Sapiens have always been very cruel and inhuman, they have often tried to dominate over other species, tribes, or even amongst peers. In ancient cultures and even not so many centuries ago, slavery was the way to have "low-cost labour" to build, to cultivate, even to teach and mentor the richest, the nobles, the aristocrats. And today? Well, we are in a situation that may seem different from a superficial point of view, but if you look at it in a deeper way, it is not. We still have very rich people, that still have to grow, and feed, and produce, and educate their progeny, their families, their peers. But, you may think, in most of the world, slavery is not permitted any more! You are correct, it's not permitted, so a solution had to be found. What if, instead of binding someone in physical slavery, you could have the same person feel unhappy, unworthy, insecure, fearful, angry, depressed, and tell the same person that to get out of those feelings, they just need to buy a new dress, or pair of shoes, or watch a TV show on their new mega TV set, or drive their fantastic car while navigating free on the internet on their smartphone? And to be able to have all these solutions, all that's needed is a little money, which can be earned working for more than half the time they are not sleeping at night... In other words, as I often explain during my seminars, in ancient Rome, the definition of a slave was someone that in exchange for his work would get fed and a place to sleep and, if he or she served their master well, they could become free as a "liberto," which means "freed." What about a worker nowadays? Well, the definition is someone that in exchange for the abilities that have been taught to them and for their time they get enough money to buy food and a house (and some anti-depressants, both as drugs and objects) and at the end of their career, might hope to be freed, going into retirement. Pretty scary, huh?

Are you now ready to embrace that path that will help you create those changes needed to become a person that lives a free life? The D-K.a.l.t. Yourself process you just read is the means for that change in your life that will set you free from the Collective Hypnosis.

This has always been the path underneath my actions throughout my whole life. And that's why my soldiers, some 21 years ago, had noticed that I was leaving something intangible but that was "more" in emotional and spiritual terms and they felt they had to acknowledge it to me.

***

To contact Marco:

c/o Accademia Dei Coach

Via S. Anselmo 98/a

Aosta

Italy

Keynote Speaker in English, French and Italian www.MarcoValerioRicci.com m.ricci@accademiadeicoach.com

Skype: ADC.Marco.Valerio.Ricci

Facebook: www.facebook.com/MarcoValerioRicciPublic

Mobile: +39 392 9432405

www.facebook.com/marcovalerio.ricci.

Jerry M. Tolle, Sr.

Jerry Tolle worked in Corporate America for 30 years with the same company. He then made the decision to leave in 2011 to start working on his own, allowing him to have the opportunity to continue working on his own building a large social media network of business with his marketing company, building business relationships and a wealthy book of business. While working full time, Jerry was able to start his first direct sales company in 2004, 5 years later in 2009, he started 2 real estate investment companies. Once he left Corporate America in 2011, Jerry decided to build 3 more businesses. Having no investors or funding, he dedicated his time and personal funds to create 6 successful businesses to carry him through retirement and beyond, creating a financial legacy for his children and grandchildren.

Jerry is married with 4 children, 6 grandchildren, and loves helping others. He is dedicated to building other businesses and entrepreneurs such as himself with his Social Media expertise and experience, Real Estate investing companies, and business building techniques. Jerry is a Graduate of Carl Albert High School, attended Rose State College, a Business Owner, Entrepreneur, and is Business Certified. Jerry's hobbies include collecting sports memorabilia, fast sports cars, riding his Harley, and spending time with his family.

How I Became the Boss at 10 years old
By Jerry Tolle M. Tolle Sr.

The change hit me at 10, and again near "retirement" at 45, when I realized I had wasted the best of my days living someone else's dream, someone else's life. I had listened to their idea of what my dreams should be, and what would be best for me, and I followed their dream, not my own.

I thought now it's time to be selfish, yes, selfish, I know it seems like a harsh word and "selfish" thing to say, but allow me to explain. You have to understand that change for me has always been a work in progress.

The first of many changes happened to me when I was only 10 years old. This is where my change began, and continues day by day.

I remember the summer of 1971, I was 10 years old growing up in Midwest City, Oklahoma. I was with my mother; a Japanese immigrant who came to the U.S. sometime after World War II. My mother and I had been at the home of one of her Japanese friends. I remember my mother's friend asked me: "Jerry-san what do you want to be when you grow up?" The first thing that came out of my mouth, of which I spoke with great excitement, was "THE BOSS." My mom and her friend laughed and said "that was a cute thing for me to say." During the drive home, my mother told me, very lovingly; "Jerry you don't want to be the boss, you need to go to school, get good grades, go to college and then get a good job." My mother was born in Tokyo, Japan on Christmas day in 1928. She was the biggest influence in my life—I loved and respected her. If I was thinking of doing anything wrong or bad, I always thought of my mother because I did not want to bring her shame or embarrass her. Reflecting on this and my youth, I now see I learned this from her culture because in Japan, you are taught at a young age to respect your parents, to bring no shame to your elders.

My mother was deeply involved in the Japanese community in Oklahoma City. My father was a hard-working blue-collar man born in South Gate, California, served in the Army and Navy, and fought in 2 wars—WWII and the Korean War. I was told he met my mother in Japan after the war had ended and moved to Phoenix, AZ. My parents didn't know anything about running a business or being business owners because both of them were hard-working middle-class workers. My father was in law enforcement in the military, and worked for the Phoenix Police Department in the 50's. He told me he left because of the pay and decided to be a truck driver and ended up moving our family to Del City, Oklahoma in 1966.

What exactly did all that mean?

Later in life, I realized I had been doing things in my life based on what others had told me of how things should be, what my career should look like, how long I should work for "the Man," etc. It dawned on me that I left myself behind. My dreams went to the wayside of never ever land, leaving my ego and pride along with it. I wasn't selfish enough, I thought. At the same time, I was not ashamed of who I was and what I had done. I knew there was more in store for me. I continued to imagine greater, to imagine doing more, helping others, and successfully creating that legacy and be the Boss. What if I went after my dreams and made more, so I could take care of my family, leaving a greater legacy behind? Allow me to develop a small snapshot of my journey, of my change, and how it made me.

I not only had to overcome rejection; fear; trauma; a broken home; adoption; near death experiences, hospitalization on more than one occasion, failed marriage; failed business; depression; anxiety; mood disorder and many more traumatic events in my life.

Picture this……….

Brought into this world by force, pain, suffering as a product of "date rape"

Adopted by a dysfunctional family, eventually ending in divorce

The Change[11]

Raised by a loving, endearing mother who did nothing but give her love and time away to others, and not to her family.

Alcoholic abusive Father, verbally and physically, suffered from PTSD

Collapsed lung at the age of 17, unable to pursue my dream of reaching the NFL

Opportunity to walk on to the field to fulfill my dream as an athlete, turned it down

Short-term memory loss due to condition and multiple concussions and head injuries

Dropped out of college

Married for the sake of living someone else's dream, ending in divorce

Fired from Corporate Job after 19 years; brought back by the Union

Fear of commitment, continually running away from my problems and fears

Invested in several MLM's and failed

Business & Joint venture, failed

Loss of over $70,000 in investments

30-year career in corporate America, ending in retirement

Foreclosure/loss of home

$20,000 Debt loss allocation from 401k Investment Portfolio

I was born in Phoenix, AZ in December of 1960, adopted in March of 1961. I was very sick as a child, born with asthma and other ailments. Technology was not like today—there was little to nothing to better my condition. My mother held me constantly so I could sleep. Two years later, my sister was adopted. My mother was college educated and had a privileged life from an upper class family; my father was raised poor. My parents worked very hard but were so different because my mother liked the finer things in life like classical music, theater, and the arts. My father loved the outdoors, hunting, fishing, and listening to country & western music. My father had a hard time dealing with what he saw in the war. Looking back, he had PTSD; he was told to drink to calm his nerves. They didn't have counseling or the support like they have today, so my father had to deal with his pain privately. I remember playing with his 2 Purple Heart medals; my father didn't tell me much about the war.

I bounced around from job to job while I was attending junior college at Oscar Rose in Midwest City, Oklahoma. From 1980-1981, I had 10 to 15 jobs. I would work a few weeks, quit, and keep trying to find a job that paid me the most money. In July 1981, I started my 30-year career in telecommunications by applying at Southwestern Bell. This was my first real taste of Corporate America. I was in training, which took 4 to 6 weeks and I called in sick because I hated the structure. My trainer, who was an elderly lady, told me as long as she had been a trainer for 25+ years, anyone who called in sick got fired. I really didn't care and thought maybe this will be my way out. As luck turned out, upper management liked me and let me stay. A few months later, they wanted to promote me to manager, but I politely told them I was only 20 years old and not really ready to take on that much responsibility. I remember meeting some people that had been with the phone company for 25 to 30 years. I laughed, made fun of them, and said I will never work 30 years and if I did last that long I would retire at 50.

My success now exists due to two vehicles of opportunity. Join me on an entrepreneur's dream of success, positivity, growth, freedom, and the obtaining the wealth you deserve.

Real Estate Investment business—TMJ ELLOT, which will help your money grow in real estate. Currently purchasing multi-units, single family homes, new builds, buy & holds, fix & flips. TMJ ELLOT is always looking to joint venture and partner up with others investors. We can show you how to create a self-directing Roth or Traditional IRA to move money from your savings, 401k, or retirement funds. TMJ ELLOT believes in investing in real estate where you can have more control of your investment. We have a system that will calculate and find deals that work best for our clients. Bottom line—the numbers have to work or we walk away.

Direct Marketing Venture—this vehicle of opportunity is for people that don't have the money to invest or perhaps are tired of working in Corporate America and eventually want to replace their J.O.B. This vehicle will help you build a business at home; you can do it full or part time. I will personally teach you a proven system that has been in place over 40+ years—all you do is follow the system that's put in place and simply duplicate. I will mentor and teach you how to build a business, paying you over and over again even while you are sleeping. I will also show you how to create a solid business where you can build it long term and receive residual income.

I know if I can endure, overcome, and become selfish, so can you.

Think about where you are in your life right now—are you ready for the change, or has it already happened, or you weren't being selfish or perhaps you didn't know how to change or that it even existed?

Know you are better, know you are worthy, know you are capable, know you are powerful and you can accomplish your dreams and what you set out to do as an entrepreneur and beautiful individual in this world.

Here's to your success, to being selfish, to making a better life for you and your family! Discover your dreams and your success through your changes in your journey.

And be the "Boss" of you, even at 10 years old and perhaps 40, 50, or whatever age it hits you.

Here is how I allowed the change to exist in me…….

I never gave up, I made a choice to become great, to be better than when I started. I read *Think and Grow Rich* in my 40's. When I read that book at that time, I realized I was practicing some of the principles it teaches. I ended up retiring in July 2011 which was 30 years from when I started and I was 50 years old. I shouted out to the universe what I wanted and ended up doing just exactly what I mentioned 30 years earlier. When I retired, I did not take a pension—I took a lump sum or buyout for my retirement, which I could not live off of or spend because I was too young to retire. I decided if I wanted to leave at 50 years old, I would need a plan, so I decided to start my own direct sales company in 2004. I also invested in myself in 2008 and went to school to learn how to do real estate investing. I started TMJ ELLOT in 2009, when I met my current business partner. I told him, "We are going to start a company when I retire in a few years." He agreed, and we created a business and JV'd in 2011.

Shortly after I left the phone company, I ended up losing my home to a foreclosure while trying to do a short sale. I moved to Utah to be closer to my daughter & grandchildren. This is where I ended up meeting the love of my life, my wife who gave me two more sons, and I now have three sons and a daughter in my life.

In the mid 2000's, so many people saw how much money you could make in real estate. Everyone wanted to be a real estate investor and rent or flip houses here in Phoenix. People didn't have any idea what they were doing and ended up losing their homes, life savings, 401k, or retirement funds. Most people failed because they had not been properly trained. I was trained on what to do by people who actually made money during the crash. This is where I can help you—TMJ ELLOT actually has a business model you follow and work on a case by case basis. Our business motto is "You have to have a certain amount of profit or we will not do the deal." Since establishment in March 2009, TMJ ELLOT has no allocated losses on an investment creating JV's with other investors. I cannot guarantee you will make any profit because as you know, any investment you decide to do carries risk. My company's very first property purchased was a

The Change[11]

multi-unit triplex acquired for $35,000 and cash-flows over $1000 monthly since purchase. My business partner and I have made an agreement to sell 3 units to another investor who had 7 units next door, adjacent to our property. An interest only loan for $15,000 cash up front, seller-financing, 3-year term, paying over $700 monthly = instant cash flow and high profit margin.

I always felt different than my parents; I had a mother who believed in me no matter what I did, then on the other hand I had a father battling his own demons inside because of the wars he fought in. My father was a very loving man when he wasn't drinking, but I rarely saw that side of my father. He was angry or drunk most of my childhood. He never believed in me and thought I was lazy because I hated to work like him. He physically & mentally abused me from the ages of 4 to 17. The breaking point was in 1978, when I was 17 years old. He ended up squeezing me so hard it punctured my lung and collapsed it, landing me in the ICU for 14 days. Soon after, just a short couple of years later, my father transferred his job to Winslow, a small town in Northern Arizona in 1980. I ended up living with my parents for less than a year and moved back to Oklahoma City to attend college. I left home at 19. I vowed to never go back home again, and I never did.

I ended up getting married in 1983, had my first child in March 1984—my baby girl. The first time I held her in my arms, I cried like a baby because I finally felt someone was a part of me. I never knew I could love someone so much until that day. My daughter was the very first person to start my healing process. Five and half years later, in December 1989, I had my second child, a little boy. I remember holding my son and feeling so proud of him. My son began another stage of healing all the pain I had from my father. I tried to do my best raising my children, but I had so much anger built up and my children had to deal with my constant outbursts.

One thing I can honestly say is my grandchildren will never see the pain or anger I had as a youth. I always tell people being a grandfather, I only have one thing in life that is to never say no to them. The birth of my two children helped ease some of my pain, but it still burned hot at times. I didn't know until later in my life I had a mood disorder where I would get angry over little silly stupid things. I yelled and screamed because I had so much hurt inside of me. I didn't know how to control it. I tried my best to be a good father, to be better than mine. I constantly told my children how proud of them I was and how much I loved them. I saw how I emotionally hurt my children growing up because I had so much pain and didn't know how to handle my feelings inside.

God has always protected me from death, from the day I was born being sick with asthma, from my first concussion when I was hit with a baseball bat on my head. When I suffered a collapsed lung and was hospitalized. Twice in the early 90's, I tried to take my life and again God spared me. In 2008, I choked on food, passed out, and my hit head on floor, sending me to the hospital once more with my second concussion, which caused me to have short-term memory loss. And most recently, after a motorcycle accident while wearing no helmet during a high impact collision, incurring severe injury, head trauma, and another concussion, my life was again restored.

When I divorced in 2005, all I did was WORK, WORK, WORK to get my businesses up and running. I worked my full-time job at the phone company, would come home, and work my part-time business. I hadn't mentioned as of yet, but I was able to locate my birth mother, sister, and brother in the 90's. I called and talked with my sister shortly after we met, finding that her and her husband were business owners. I asked my sister if our family held jobs or were they business owners. She shared the history of my heritage with me, also divulging the fact that most of our family were entrepreneurs, and it hit me, it was starting to make perfect sense of why I always wanted to be the boss and have my own business, and why at an early age, I wanted to be the BOSS at a mere 10 years old, even when I didn't know what it meant at the time. Meeting my siblings and birth mother in my early to late 30's started to slowly let me begin to forgive my father, whose approval I had so desperately wanted. My youngest grandson was named after my

The Change[11]

father by his grandson who he never met, my son. When I see my youngest grandson, I think of my father and wonder if he was still alive today if he would be proud of me and what I have accomplished in my life. We all have pain or hurt inside because of others. Just remember to forgive those who have hurt you. Think of it like this: the only reason people do what they do is because someone or something placed that pain into them. It's really not entirely their fault. By forgiving people who hurt you, you will only heal you.

I have had a lot of negative things happen to me, but I have never given up on my dream of being a business owner. I simply had to go through the change to get me there. I had to overcome so much in my life and I still struggle today. I have been blessed with strong women in my life, my mother and my wife. Besides the love and support I received from my mother, my wife has made me better later in my life. I had so much pain and didn't know how to handle my problems. It took me over 30 years to find a woman who loves me for me. I thank God for putting my wife in my life because she was the final piece of my healing process. She has taught me to be calm, patience, trust people who love me, and have balance in my life. I wouldn't be the man I am today if it wasn't for these two strong women. My mother was my personal life coach. I watched how she served others, loved, helped, and put others first. When I was little, my mother would always tell me this story with tears in her eyes— she would say Jerry, you are very special. I personally picked you and God has blessed me with two angels. My wife is the balance in my life, she calms my soul and continues to trust and believe in me creating my balance.

I remember talking to a friend right after my divorce in 2005. He told me that my father made me the man I was today. I was so angry at him. I couldn't believe he had the nerve to say that to me. He had nothing to do with the man I was today. I did it all myself. My friend wanted to explain. He said I did everything opposite of my father. I was with my children every day, loved my children, told them daily how much they meant to me. Worked hard to build my businesses and teach them how to be successful. After I thought about it, he was right—my father did make me the man I am today. I did everything opposite of my father. I was able to start my first business in 2004, built 2 more businesses in 2009 and 3 more after I retired from Corporate America in 2012 after working 30 years with the same company.

Many have asked me if there is anything you could change what would it be; I tell them NOTHING. I wouldn't be me or have all these people I love in my life if something changed. It took me 30 years to be a CEO, but I can truly say I am blessed and today I really am the BOSS.

My success and dream of being the boss has created fortune as I have had to overcome these obstacles in life, creating an entrepreneur's dream like TMJ ELLOT. Let me help you grow your investments through real estate investing or through our second vehicle working at home, where I can show you how to build a successful business, so you can have the TIME, FREEDOM, & INCOME to live your life on your own terms. Don't do it backwards like I did and wait 25+ years to make a change. You can invest with TMJ ELLOT http://www.tmjellot.com or build a successful home based business with a proven system http://www.jerrytolle.com

My personal must-haves in accomplishing aspirations in life, dreams, and becoming a successful entrepreneur and business owner:

Support

System

Mentor

Family & Friends

Desire to Succeed

Believing in yourself

The Change[11]

Change is what I look forward to in my life, in my business at home. If it weren't for change, I wouldn't be where I am, who I am, and be what I am today. Embrace the change in your life and in your business and be the boss of you. I didn't start out with the best of odds. It is difficult for me to share my darkness with you, but rewarding at the same time because of how far I have come and with this I hope you too can face your battles, overcome your obstacles, rise above your pain, and make the best of what you have started with and end even greater and better than when you began, and along the way bring as many with you in your journey to succeed, paving a grand path for others to follow in order to be the change to success as an entrepreneur. Remember, it's not how you began, but how you chose to finish, and I will finish strong. I know you will too.

In closing, I will leave you with a few "Jerryisms" as my wife would call them.

"The day you finally decide you don't need someone's constant approval or opinion is the first day of your new life."

"People too weak to follow their dreams will always find a way to discover your dream."

"It's your choice if you want to suffer or be mediocre; we weren't put on earth to be average."

"Just remember your checking account balance doesn't define who you are."

"You know it really comes down to either you believe you can do it, or you just quit, whichever is easier, have some faith in yourself"

***

To contact Jerry:

email: info@tmjellot.com

https://www.facebook.com/jerrymtollesr

info@tmjellot.com

WWW.TMJELLOT.COM

(480) 818-8485

George Lynch

George Lynch has a passion for helping others and understands that you must have passion in your life. He understands you must push through every "NO" you get in life and turn it into a lesson on how to achieve "YES."

At the age of 24, George is an aspiring speaker and currently a mentor focused on young adults from high school, college, sports, as well as in life and business.

A quote George lives by is "You can overcome anything you undergo." He plans to help others to understand anything is possible. If you want something bad enough, you can achieve it.

When you meet George, you will understand he has learned gifts come in unusual wrapping. He believes passion and understanding life's lessons are words which we all should live by.

I cannot fit all of my life experiences or the ways I dealt with them in this chapter. If you want to learn more ways to improve yourself as a person, I am willing to speak and mentor in all parts of the world. Reach out to me and I would love to show you how.

The Diamond Kid

By George Lynch

At first, a diamond is just a rock in the dirt. Pressure makes diamonds; we were all made to shine. The pressures and obstacles life puts us through are only molding us into a beautiful diamond.

I've learned to be like water, and also not to expect help and that is when life becomes easier. I learned that at an early stage in my life. In most people's eyes, I was never going to shine, but I always knew I was a diamond in the rough. Growing up, there were many obstacles I had to deal with, but like how water reacts, I knew I could get around them. Some of the obstacles I had to deal with were exterior and interior. The exterior obstacles in my life were being told I would never finish school, getting turned back when trying to attend college, and being mistreated by the police. Also getting looked over as a person and athlete. The biggest obstacles in my life was the interior one, which was me being in my own way.

"You are going to be in school till you are gray."

That is what was said to me by my grandmother as young boy. Hearing those words made me think less of myself and feel very dark inside. Growing up, school was no cakewalk for me because of that; I was not a fan of school. I never understood what the teacher was saying or showing me. This also caused me not to like books. Back then, reading a book was like taking a fish out of water to me and I thought it was going to kill me. I could not read and numbers went right over my head. I have two vivid memories of my childhood I will never forget. One is the day a teacher asked me to read aloud in class. I felt like a singer on stage, the spotlight was on me. I told the teacher I did not want to read, but he kept insisting I did. He would not take no for an answer. It got to the point that I ran out of the classroom crying. Another time I will always remember is the day my mother and I were on the bus and I was trying to read different signs on the bus. One of the signs I was trying to read was actually in Spanish and I did not know. My reading was so bad I did not know I was trying to read a different language. School was so difficult for me I had summer school every summer in order to move up to the next grade. The fact I could not read weighed heavily upon me. With hard work and dedication, I learned to read very well and graduated both high school and college. Don't ever let anybody tell you what you can and can't do. The things people tell you do not have to be the totality of your life.

"Put your head down and keep working."

It was the last day of my college basketball tryouts and I had given it everything I had. To play college basketball was a childhood dream of mine. I had dedicated countless hours and many long nights in the NYC parks and gyms to basketball. I had been waiting for this moment all my life. I stood in the hallway anticipating what was waiting for me on the other side of the wall. Sweaty palms, heart beating rapidly, and pacing back and forth as I tried to keep a level head. The door to the coach's office opened and my name was called. As I walked into the office, my mind was hell-bent on the hopes the next words to come out of the coach's mouth were "you made that team." I stood across from the three coaches as I was told how tough of a player I was. The words that followed after were "George I can't cut you, but as far as making the team, it's a NO. But you can practice and travel with us if you want." The room went completely silent as I looked at the coach as his mouth was moving, but I could not hear anything he was saying. It was as if everything in my world had stopped. As I snapped back into realty, I told the coach I would still love to practice and travel with the team. This was hard to swallow, but my passion for the game did not allow me to turn down the offer. In addition, this was bigger than me—I just wanted to be a part of a team and family. Not everybody is going to see your true value, but you have to know your true value.

"You made me run. You are going to jail. And you know what happens to people in jail?"

The Change[11]

Those were some of the things said to me by the police officers while I was cuffed in a police van, bloody and beaten. It was a hot summer night just after I walked my then girlfriend home. Before that night, I had never been in trouble with the police. As I made my way back home, I ran into few people I knew from playing basketball in the park. They were all in front of a house just sitting and talking. I stopped and began talking with them. After a few minutes, a police van pulled up. The driver of the van asked, "Do any of you live here?" I was not sure if any of the guys lived there, so I didn't say anything, but one of the guys said, "Yes. My friend does." I was not sure if that was true or not. After that, the officer on the passenger said asked, "Are you guys kidding me?" and jumped out of the van aggressively. Remember before this I had never had a run in with the police. So I did not know what to do or what was about to happen. Growing up, my mother always warned me about the police. With my mother's voice in the back of my head and not having an ID, maybe I should not, but I ran. I only had on shorts, a shirt, socks, and slippers.

After taking off running, for a minute or two there were no cops in sight. I found myself in a dark backyard. Just blocks away from my house where I was trying to go. After a few minutes of being in the backyard and not seeing a cop, I decided it was safe to come out and keep heading home. How stupid was I—here I had the biggest gang in New York City after me. As I made my way closer to my house, there was a cop car. They saw me, said "there he goes," and I took off running. Now I was a fugitive on the run in the middle of the Bronx, where crime was high. I continued running and there were cops everywhere, cops in cars and on foot. As I ran, a cop running behind me said, "Stop or I'm going to shoot." What he said did not register at the moment; I was too scared to stop running. I end up hopping a gate into a dark driveway and backyard. There was nowhere else to run and at that point, an officer was right behind me. I was then taken down to the ground, hands put behind my back. As I was face down on the ground in handcuffs, an officer stood over me and said, "You made me run." Then I was kicked in the face. I was then hit a few more times by that officer or another one. After being beaten and threatened, I was put in the back of a police van. I sat in the back of the police van feeling scared and alone, as if I was just kidnapped. I was covered in so much blood I could smell and taste it. These were not like small cuts you get from falling. My clothes had been all torn and my face was covered in blood. I was threatened some more and even told, "We found a gun—you are going to jail."

I was taken to the police precinct, unsure what would happen. I was called names and made fun of. I remember one officer saying "oh you are slippers." I was then walked into a room where I was asked if I wanted any medical care. After being asked that, one of the officers said getting medical care would only make my processing longer. If I wanted things to go faster, I shouldn't have them take me to the ER. I was fingerprinted and put in a holding cell. I sat in the holding cell the rest of the night. At one point, I was asked by an officer if I wanted any food or anything. I stayed there till the next morning, when I was released 8 hours after. It was the longest 8 hours of my life not knowing what the outcome would be. A female officer walked me out of the precinct and said to me, "I don't know what happened because I wasn't your arresting officer, but you are free to go and if you don't tell your mother what happened we won't be contacting her so she doesn't have to know about this." She then went on to say there were no charges against me. I then went home and was taken to the ER to find out I had suffered a fractured nose and shoulder, with a few other bruises. Most people would have let that be the end-all tell-all situation of their life. But I didn't let that situation define me. What doesn't kill you only makes you stronger

"Remember your WHY"

I was excited it was the morning before I would take off for college. I gathered all my belongings, which was three small bags and a large suitcase. I made my way downtown to Port Authority on the 6 train from the Bronx. I found my bus. It was a tight hot and sweaty Greyhound. The ride was about 5 to 6 hours. When I arrived to the campus, I was welcomed by the fresh air. I could smell the freshly cut grass and hear the beautiful birds chirping. The biggest shock for me was seeing the deer. I had never seen a deer in person before that day. I made my way into the college and up to the admissions office, where I met the director. He walked me into this office and said "have a seat George." We talked about the weather and my ride up to the college. As he went through my file, that's when he said the gut-wrenching words: "George we have a problem, I do not have your immunization papers. Without that, I can't put you in a dorm." I looked at him in disbelief, asking if he was sure. He said that since I wouldn't be able to stay on campus, I was going to have to head back home. There was nothing I could do, so I got back on the next bus and went back another 6 hours home. I didn't let it defeat me, though, because I remembered my WHY. I went back home, got the paperwork I needed, and looked to head back up to school.

It was the night before my bus left and things only became harder for me. It's true what they say "everything gets worse before it gets better. So when you feel like quitting, remember why you started." I called a good friend of mine and asked him if he could drop me at the bus station the next morning. I had too many bags to take the public train again and also I did not want there to be a chance of me missing the bus. If you know anything about the New York City train system, they aren't very reliably when it comes to time. Unfortunately, his reply was that he couldn't because he had to work in the morning, but he could take me that night. I agreed and told him to come get me soon. It was about 11 o'clock when he showed up. We drove downtown to Port Authority. I unloaded my bags, and went inside and found where my bus would be leaving the next morning. I don't remember the gate number, but that's where I slept that night right in the New York City Port Authority Bus Station. I felt cold, alone, and uncomfortable, but I knew better days were ahead. I knew I was one more bad situation closer to being successful. If you want the rainbow, you have to take the rain.

"Who's in control"

I wanted to be in control of my own life and destiny. It was time to run on my own energy—enough was enough. The coaches, my grandmother, and the world ought not to dictate my life. I told myself this and have never looked back since. I took some time to sit down and ask myself what was my personal legend. After some deep soul searching, it hit me—I'm most happy when helping others. My purpose in the world was to impact as many lives as possible in a positive way. It's a feeling I get from helping others, I can't put it into words. How am I'm going to follow my personal legend and better myself and others? Lightbulb moment. Being an entrepreneur is the way to do it. I learned in an entrepreneur class that to be a great entrepreneur, you have to solves problems or improve people's lives. When those two thing are done, the rest will take care of itself, as far as making money or anything along those lines. There was one more obstacle in the way of my success.

"You are your worst own enemy."

"George, you are standing in your own way of being successful." This was the much needed conversation I had with myself. It took some time, but that's something I said to myself. "You are stopping yourself from becoming the best and most successful person possible." I didn't believe in myself and I was letting the world push me around. The world was not just pushing me around, but I wasn't educating myself either. I began reading more books and researching successful entrepreneurs and their path to success. Also, I didn't hold myself to a high enough standard. By procrastinating and using words such as *if*, *maybe*, *hope*, *can't*, and *try* were ways I was in my own way. Lastly, I didn't think about the people around me and all I could offer them; I was being selfish. I didn't understand that things were bigger then me and there were many people counting on me. So if you see yourself doing any of those things, do the world and yourself a huge favor and stop. You are a special and unique person who has a lot to offer the world. If you have no enemy within, the enemy outside cannot hurt you.

The Change[11]

"Your body only goes as far as you mind takes it."

My mindset the whole time was to never give up or take no for an answer. I may just be a kid from the south Bronx, but I had something to offer the world. Also, I decided not to let myself or anything get in the way of me being the best and most successful person possible. I always reminded myself that I can overcome anything I undergo. I also always kept in my mind that if I didn't believe in myself, nobody else would. The lesson here is only you can dictate how your life flows. There is a famous quote by Bruce Lee: "Empty your mind, be formless, shapeless like water. If you put water in the cup, it becomes the cup and water can flow or it can crash." I was formless, shapeless like water, and did not let any of those situation dictate my life. So empower yourself and have a mindset similar to mine and anything is possible. Here I am the kid no one expected to shine. I've graduated both high school and college. Have orchestrated events for a business startup and was an ambassador of my college. The same director that sent me back home that day later offered me the position as ambassador. I'm now 24 and have empowered myself to do things I didn't even see myself doing. I have my own car and apartment and been blessed to say I own stocks in three major companies. I'm also a licensed real estate agent, looking to own property very soon. It hasn't been easy to get where I am and it won't be easy to get where I want to be. I can tell you one thing—here's a quote by me, George J. Lynch: "You can overcome anything you undergo." If I can do it, you can do it too, just believe in yourself.

I did have help from countless people along the way. To many to name them all, but there are some who really impacted my life in a huge way. Russell Man Robison of the GoalGetters who is a coach, mentor, and father figure. Also Evander Ford, coach of Ford Tough, a coach and grandfather to me, and Harris Friess of the Brooklyn Sports Youth Club, coach and mentor to me.

***

To contact George:

Phone (518) 844-4095

Email george.lynch93@yahoo.com

https://www.linkedin.com/m/?sessionid=7989779121569792#

Facebook https://m.facebook.com/george.lynch.12?ref=bookmarks

AFTERWORD

Life is always a series of transitions... people, places, and things that shape who we are as individuals. Often, you never know that the next catalyst for change is around the corner.

Jim Britt and Jim Lutes have spent decades influencing individuals to blossom into the best version of themselves.

Allow all you have read in this book to create introspection and redirection if required. It's your journey to craft.

The Change is a series. A global movement. Watch for future releases and add them to your collection. If you know of anyone who would like to be considered as a co-author for a future book, have them email our offices at support@jimbritt.com.

The individual and combined works of Jim Britt and Jim Lutes have filled seminar rooms to maximum capacity and created a worldwide demand.

The blessings go both ways, as Jim and Jim are always willing students of life. Out of demand for life-changing programs and events, Jim and Jim conduct seminars and keynote presentations worldwide.

To Schedule Jim Britt or Jim Lutes as your featured speaker at your next convention or special event, or to organize and host a seminar in your area, email: support@jimbritt.com

Master your moment as they become hours that become days.

Your legacy awaits.

All the best,

Jim Britt and Jim Lutes

www.ingramcontent.com/pod-product-compliance
Lightning Source LLC
Chambersburg PA
CBHW070559300426
44113CB00010B/1316